RANKS AND UNIFORMS OF THE GERMAN ARMY, NAVY AND AIR FORCE

By
DENYS ERLAM

Collected from German Semi-official Sources and largely based upon

UNIFORMEN
DER DEUTSCHEN WEHRMACHT

by

EBERHARD HETTLER

of the German Air Ministry

The Naval & Military Press Ltd

Published by

The Naval & Military Press Ltd
Unit 10 Ridgewood Industrial Park,
Uckfield, East Sussex,
TN22 5QE England

Tel: +44 (0) 1825 749494
Fax: +44 (0) 1825 765701

www.naval-military-press.com
www.nmarchive.com

In reprinting in facsimile from the original, any imperfections are inevitably reproduced and the quality may fall short of modern type and cartographic standards.

INTRODUCTION

THE SUPREME COMMANDER of the Armed Forces or *Wehrmacht* is the Führer and Chancellor, Adolf Hitler.

His staff, known as the High Command of the *Wehrmacht*, is presided over by his Chief-of-Staff. Following them in seniority comes the " Supreme Court of the Armed Forces ".

The *Wehrmacht* embraces the three Services : the Army, Navy and Air Force, each of which has its own Commander-in-Chief, the German equivalent of the Commander-in-Chief of the Air Force holding at the same time the office of Minister for Air.

THE UNIFORMS OF THE ARMED FORCES

As in our own Fighting Forces, each of the Services has its characteristic uniform which has been historically evolved, but in the *Wehrmacht* of to-day there are three badges which appear on every uniform : the Cockade surrounded by oak-leaves, worn on the cap-band, the emblem of Nazi Germany, worn above the Cockade, and the same badge embroidered on the right breast.

Since it has been adopted as the national emblem, the eagle and swastika are sometimes incorporated in the uniforms of other State organizations, but, by law, it may be worn on the right breast only by members of the three Fighting Services.

CONTENTS

PART I: THE ARMY

THE ACTIVE LIST	page 11
THE RESERVE	13
GERMAN RANKS AND THEIR BRITISH EQUIVALENTS	14
WAFFENFARBEN	17
BADGES OF RANK: PRIVATES, N.C.O.s AND W.O.s	20
OFFICERS	21
MEDICAL AND VETERINARY	22
REGIMENTAL BANDS	24
FORTIFICATION W.O.s	24
ORDNANCE	25
WEHRMACHTBEAMTEN	26
COLLAR AND CUFF PATCHES	27
AIGUILLETTES	29
SHOULDER-STRAPS FOR N.C.O.s AND MEN	30
THE MODERN UNIFORM	35
THE STEEL HELMET	36
UNIFORM CAPS	38
UNIFORM TUNICS	42
UNIFORMS OF MECHANIZED TROOPS	47
GREAT-COATS	49
ARMY CHAPLAINS	51
TROUSERS	53
BOOTS	54
SPECIALIST BADGES	55

CONTENTS

MARKSMAN'S LANYARD	page 57
STANDARD BEARERS	58
"SWALLOWS' NESTS"	58
MOUNTAIN GUIDES	59
FAUSTRIEMEN AND *TRODDELN*	60
SIDE-ARMS	63

PART II: THE NAVY

THE UNIFORMS	69
ORGANIZATION	70
CADETS AND MIDSHIPMEN	70
ACTIVE OFFICERS	71
MARINEBEAMTEN	72
NAVY RANKS AND THEIR BRITISH NAVAL AND GERMAN ARMY EQUIVALENTS	73
BADGES OF RANK: P.O.s AND MEN	74
CADETS	77
MIDSHIPMEN	78
OFFICERS	79
MUSICIANS	82
UNIFORM CAPS	84
UNIFORMS OF P.O.s AND MEN	87
UNIFORMS OF WARRANT OFFICERS	90
UNIFORMS OF OFFICERS	91
GREAT-COATS	95
AIGUILLETTES	96
CHAPLAINS	97
GLOVES AND SHOES	97
SPECIALIST BADGES	98
MARKSMAN'S LANYARD	100
SIDE-ARMS AND *PORTEPEES*	102
FIELD-GREY UNIFORM	103
UNIFORM CAPS	104
SHOULDER-STRAPS FOR P.O.s AND MEN	105

PART III: THE AIR FORCE

The New *Luftwaffe*	page 109
The Organization	110
Ranks of the *Luftwaffe* and their R.A.F. Equivalents	112
Waffenfarben	113
Badges of Rank: Men	114
N.C.O.s and W.O.s	115
Officers	116
Corps of Engineers	119
Navigational Corps	120
Medical Corps	120
Musicians	120
Shoulder-Straps	121
Specialist Badges	123
Marksman's Lanyard	125
Standard Bearers	126
Musicians	127
Commemoration Armlets	127
Uniforms	128
Steel Helmets	130
Uniform Caps	130
Tunics	132
Flying Tunic	134
Aiguillettes	137
Coats and Cloaks	138
Working Uniform	140
Flying Kit	140
Waterproof Coat	142
Mountain Equipment	143
Parachute Troops; Special Equipment	143
Faustriemen and *Portepees*	144
Side-Arms	145
Trousers	146
Footwear	146
GLOSSARY	151

LIST OF ILLUSTRATIONS IN COLOUR

PLATE 1   *Frontispiece*
1. GENERAL OF INFANTRY. *Full Dress.*—2. LIEUTENANT-GENERAL. *Parade Dress. (Order: Grand Cross of the Crown of Italy.)*—3. COLONEL OF INFANTRY. *Parade Dress.*—4. STAFF-CAPTAIN. *Undress Uniform with Piped Field Service Tunic.*—5. CAPTAIN OF ARTILLERY. *Field Dress with Field Service Cap*

PLATE 2   To Face page 16
1. CAPTAIN, *Army Medical Corps. Full Dress.*—2. SECOND-LIEUTENANT, *Tank Corps. Parade Dress.*—3. SECOND-LIEUTENANT, *Smoke Troops. Undress Uniform with Piped Field Service Tunic.*—4. REGIMENTAL SERGEANT-MAJOR, *Cavalry. Parade Dress.*—5. REGIMENTAL SERGEANT-MAJOR, *Signal Corps*

PLATE 3   To Face page 32
1. SENIOR OFFICIAL, *Air Ministry. Walking-out Dress.*—2. MAJOR, *Veterinary Corps. Walking-out Dress.*—3. OFFICIAL, *Naval Commissariat. Undress Uniform.*—4. ARMY CHAPLAIN. *Walking-out Dress.*—5. SERGEANT-MAJOR, *Fire-fighting Branch of the Air Force*

PLATE 4   To Face page 48
1. PRIVATE, *6th Regiment Tank Corps.*—2. LANCE-SERGEANT. *Smoke Screen Instruction and Research Section.*—3. ACTING SERGEANT-MAJOR, *4th Regiment Tank Corps.*—4. MAJOR, *7th Cavalry Regiment. Undress Uniform with Piped Field Service Tunic.*—5. OFFICIAL, *Commissariat Department. Lieutenant*

PLATE 5   To Face page 64
1. SERGEANT-MAJOR, *Mountain Regiment. Walking-out Dress.*—2. LANCE-CORPORAL, *Artillery. Walking-out Dress (former Austrian Army Tunic).*—3. SENIOR PRIVATE, *Infantry Regiment. Field Service Dress.*—4. SAPPER. *Parade Dress.*—5. JAEGER (*Private*), *Mountain Regiment. Field Service Dress*

ILLUSTRATIONS IN COLOUR

PLATE 6   To Face page 72
1. REAR-ADMIRAL. *Full Dress. (Order: Hungarian Order of Merit, 1st Class).*—2. CAPTAIN *(acting Commodore). Full Dress with Frock Coat.*—3. LIEUTENANT. *Full Dress with Mess Jacket.*—4. ENGINEER-LIEUTENANT. *Service Dress.*—5. SUB-LIEUTENANT, *Marine Artillery. Field Service Dress*

PLATE 7   To Face page 88
1. SIGNAL PETTY OFFICER. *Service Dress. Fleet Command.*— 2. QUARTERMASTER. *Service Dress as Watchkeeping Warrant Officer.*—3. LIEUTENANT COMMANDER, *Marine Artillery. Service Dress.*—4. COMMANDER. *Field Grey Service Dress.*— 5. ADMIRAL. *Full Dress with Aiguillettes*

PLATE 8   To Face page 104
1. QUARTERMASTER. *(Warrant Officer.) Service Dress.*— 2. CHIEF PETTY OFFICER *(Engine-room). Service Dress.*— 3. CHIEF PETTY OFFICER, *Marine Artillery. Field Service Dress.*—4. ABLE SEAMAN. *Shore Parade Dress.*—5. ABLE SEAMAN SIGNALLER. *Landing Rig*

PLATE 9   To Face page 112
1. GENERAL OF THE AIR FORCE. *Parade Dress. (Order: Grand Cross of the Crown of Italy.)*—2. GROUP CAPTAIN. *Formal Full Dress (Evening).*—3. SQUADRON LEADER, *Signals. Parade Dress.*—4. SQUADRON LEADER, *General Staff.*—5. SURGEON FLIGHT-LIEUTENANT. *Undress Uniform with White Coat*

PLATE 10   To Face page 128
1. SECOND-LIEUTENANT, *Anti-Aircraft Artillery. Formal Dress (Evening).*—2. PILOT OFFICER. *Undress Uniform with Forage Cap.* —3. DRUM-MAJOR, *General Goering Regiment. Parade Dress.*—4. SERGEANT-PILOT. *Walking-out Dress.*—5. SERGEANT, *Anti-Aircraft Artillery. Field Service Dress with Forage Cap*

PLATE 11   To Face page 144
1. AIRCRAFTMAN. *(1st Class.) General Goering Regiment. Field Dress with Uniform Tunic.*—2. SENIOR WARRANT OFFICER, *Flying Branch. Parade Dress.*—3. PILOT OFFICER, *1st Parachute Regiment. Parade Dress.*—4. GROUP-CAPTAIN, *Air Ministry. Parade Dress.*—5. MARSHAL OF THE AIR FORCE. *Parade Dress*

PART I

THE ARMY

THE ARMY

COMPOSITION OF THE ARMY

The Active List

Men and N.C.O.s

THE MEN ON the Active List comprising the ranks are of two distinct types : those who are in the Army for the purpose of performing their military service, and enlisted men who have signed-on for a period of years.

N.C.O.s—known, from Corporal to Sergeant, as *Unteroffiziere ohne Portepee*—and Warrant Officers, from Sergeant-Major onwards, as *Unteroffiziere mit Portepee*—are appointed in the usual way except that, when considering a man for promotion, the German mind attaches more importance to length of service than we do. Even in wartime, when sensational advancement is no novelty to us, suitability for a higher position is not sufficient qualification in itself. The applicant must show that he has served the period specified as necessary for the promotion in question. Exception is made only when, by reason of *force majeure*, no one with the necessary record is available. This applies also to Officers.

Ensigns

Serving in the ranks, first as a junior N.C.O., and subsequently in grades equivalent to Sergeant, Sergeant-Major and Warrant Officer, is the *Fähnrich* or Ensign. An embryo Officer, he has no parallel in our own Army, but corresponds in some ways to an *Aspirant* in the French Forces. His only privilege while serving as a junior N.C.O. is that he is allowed to wear the *portepee* or side-arm tassel, otherwise granted only to Officers and Warrant Officers.

Officers

Officers may also be sub-divided into two groups—regular and *Ergänzungs* officers.

An *Ergänzungs* Officer is a regular, who, after having retired, has been re-employed. His uniform is not in any way different from those of his brother-Officers (except when he is attached to the High Command; *Ergänzungs* Officers do not wear the special uniform of the High Command), but he is not subject to the general regulations relating to promotion, etc.

Administrative Officials or " Wehrmachtbeamten "

Officials employed in the various Ministries and Government Departments connected with the Services, who, in this country, would rate definitely as civilians, in Germany are uniformed and given military rank.

It might be argued that, if one walks through one of our own Ministries, one might easily meet someone in uniform who is employed there. There is, however, a difference.

The *Wehrmachtbeamter* is not necessarily a regular Officer of the Army employed in an administrative position because, for example, of special knowledge. Except for the compulsory military service that everyone must do, he may never have been active at all. There is no parallel in the British Army, except, possibly, in war-time, when certain specialists are given commissioned rank to assist them in their work. So definitely are these officials (although included in the *Wehrmacht*) regarded as separate from the Army proper that, should a soldier be appointed to a position as *Wehrmachtbeamter*, he must first resign from the Active List, although he may remain on the Reserve.

The Reserve and " Zur Verfügung " Lists

Corresponding to some extent to our own Reserve are the Officers and Men of the " *Beurlaubtenstand* ". Their uniform is similar to that of the active soldier. They are, in fact, indistinguishable from the Regular Army except in official correspondence, on visiting cards, etc., when they use the letters d.R. (*der Reserve*) or d.L. (*der Landwehr*).

Regular Officers and Officers of the Reserve who have retired but are still available for the Army in time of war are said to z.V.—*zur Verfügung* (roughly " When Required ").

When z.V. Officers are detailed for duty, they become z.D. (for Disposition), and are then subject to the same rules relating to uniform as *Ergänzungs* Officers.

The Retired List

Retired Officers may apply for the right to wear the uniform of their old regiment. If permission is granted, they wear a special badge indicating that they are no longer active. When a Field Officer on the Retired List is given honorary Command of a Regiment, however, he wears the uniform of a regular Officer of his own rank.

German Ranks and their Equivalents in the British Army

The table which follows will give some idea of how the German Army ranks stand in relation to our own. It is not always possible, however, to find an exact equivalent ; since the reorganization of the *Wehrmacht* under the National-Socialists, several additional ranks have been added. In such cases an approximation has been made.

THE ARMY

	GERMAN	ENGLISH
MEN	*Schütze*	Private
	Jäger	Private (Jäger Regt. or Mountain Regt.)
	Reiter	Trooper
	Kanonier	Gunner
	Pionier	Sapper
	Funker	Signaller
	Fahrer	Driver
	Kraftfahrer	Driver (mechanized)
	Sanitätssoldat	Medical Orderly
	Beschlagschmiedschütze	Farrier
	Oberschütze	Senior Private*
	Oberreiter etc.	Senior Trooper, etc.
	Gefreiter	Lance-Corporal
	Fahnenjunker-Gefreiter	Cadet Lance-Corporal*
	Sanitätsgefreiter etc.	Lance-Corporal (Medical Corps, etc.)
N.C.O.S (*Unteroffiziere ohne Portepee*)	*Obergefreiter*	Corporal
	Beschlagschmiedsobergefreiter etc.	Farrier-Corporal, etc.
	Unteroffizier	Lance-Sergeant
	Sanitätsunteroffizier	Lance-Sergeant (Medical Corps)
	Fahnenjunkerunteroffizier etc.	Cadet Lance-Sergeant, etc.*
	Unterfeldwebel	Sergeant (Infantry, Engineers, Tank Corps, etc.)
	Unterwachmeister	Sergeant (Cavalry, Artillery, etc.)
	Fähnrich	Ensign

* Ranks used as English equivalents do not necessarily exist in the British forces.

	GERMAN	ENGLISH
WARRANT OFFICERS (*Unteroffiziere mit Portepee*)	*Feldwebel*	Company Sergeant-Major (Infantry, Engineers, etc.)
	Wachmeister	Sergeant-Major (Cavalry, Artillery, etc.)
	Beschlagmeister	Farrier Sergeant-Major
	Feuerwerker	Ordnance Serjeant-Major
	Brieftaubenmeister etc.	Pigeon Postmaster, etc.
	Oberfeldwebel Oberwachmeister etc.	Battalion Sergeant-Major
	Oberfähnrich etc.	Senior Ensign, etc.
	Hauptfeldwebel Hauptwachmeister etc.	Regimental Sergeant-Major
	Stabsfeldwebel etc.	Staff Sergeant-Major, etc.
OFFICERS	*Leutnant*	Second-Lieutenant
	Assistenzarzt	Second-Lieutenant (Medical Corps)
	Oberleutnant Oberarzt etc.	Lieutenant
	Hauptmann	Captain
	Rittmeister	Captain (Cavalry)
	Stabsarzt	Captain (Medical Corps)
	Stabsveterinär etc.	Captain (Veterinary Corps, etc.)
	Major Oberstabsarzt etc.	Major
	Oberstleutnant	Lieutenant-Colonel
	Oberfeldarzt	Lieutenant-Colonel (Medical Corps)

THE ARMY

	GERMAN	ENGLISH
OFFICERS	*Oberst* *Oberstarzt etc.*	Colonel
	Generalmajor *Generalarzt etc.*	Major-General
	Generalleutnant *Generalstabsarzt etc.*	Lieutenant-General
	General der Infanterie, Kavallerie, Artillerie, etc.	General of the Infantry, Cavalry, Artillery, etc.
	Generaloberst	General
	Generalfeldmarschall	Field-Marshal

"WAFFENFARBEN"

Throughout this book you will find frequent references to the *Waffenfarbe* in describing uniforms. Since it is a composite word without an equivalent in English and would require in translation a phrase of three or four words every time it is used, I intend to employ it in the original. Perhaps it would be well, therefore, to explain it straight away.

Literally, *Waffen*, short for *Waffengatung*, means Arm of the Service, *farbe* colour, and the origin of the word is this.

In 1900 Germany decided to send troops to China; it was during the time of the Boxer Rising. When the Expeditionary Force left for the East, they wore on their uniforms, for the first time, certain decorations in colours representing the different branches of the Service. The custom has been continued and somewhere on every uniform the *Waffenfabe* appears in one form or another. A detailed description of how it is used will be given later, but, in the meantime, perhaps it will be sufficient to outline the general allocation of the colours. It is as follows:

White . . .	Infantry
Lemon Yellow . .	Signals
Yellow . . .	Cavalry
Orange . . .	Recruiting Officers
Bright Red . .	Artillery and Generals, including Medical and Veterinary Officers of that Rank
Rose . . .	Armoured Troops
Carmine . . .	General Staff, Officers of the High Command and Veterinary Corps
Dark Red . .	Smoke Troops
Light Blue . .	Mechanized Troops
Cornflower Blue . .	Medical Corps
Light Green . .	Jäger Battalions and Mountain Jäger Regiments
Dark Green . .	Administrative Officials
Black . . .	Engineers

Although all Administrative Officials or *Wehrmachtbeamten* (with the exception of Chaplains) wear the *Waffenfarbe* dark green, in order that they can be distinguished from each other, each branch is given a second colour which is used as piping on the collar

THE ARMY 19

and cuff patches and as a second underlay on the shoulder-straps. This is how these colours are apportioned :

Carmine	All Permanent Officials of the High Command; all Education Officials, Surveyors, Librarians, Archivists, Officials of the War Research Institute, and Army History Officials of the Army Museums; Meteorological Officials; Physical Instructors; Records Officials attached to the various Commands
Bright Red	Officials of District Administrations (Commissariat Officials)
Dark Red	Officials of the Military Supreme Court
Light Blue	Military Law Officials
Light Green	Apothecary Officials (except Apothecary Warrant Officers—being soldiers they wear the cornflower-blue of the Medical Corps)
White	Army Paymaster Officials, other than those serving a District Administration (*Wehrkreis*); other Garrison and Victualling Officials
Black	Technical Officials (Building, Engineering, Armoury, etc.)
Yellow	Remount Officials
Light Brown	Non-technical specialists at Army Schools
Orange	Recruiting Office Officials

Badges of Rank

N.C.O.'s and men of the German Army show their ranks in two ways. Privates and Corporals wear their badges on the left upper arm.

SENIOR PRIVATE   LANCE-CORPORAL   CORPORAL WITH
LESS   MORE
THAN 6 YEARS' SERVICE

Braid and star are of silvered fabric (the star may be hand-embroidered on non-issue tunics, i.e. those supplied by the men themselves, usually of better material and cut, for walking-out, etc.).

Lance-Sergeants, Sergeants and Sergeants-Major wear shoulder-straps edged with silver braid.

LANCE-SERGEANT   SERGEANT AND ENSIGN
(the Number in " Waffenfarbe ")   *(Ensign : Numbers in metal)*
(Others in " Waffenfarbe ")

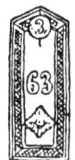  

SERGEANT-MAJOR   REGIMENTAL SERGEANT-MAJOR SENIOR ENSIGN   STAFF SERGEANT-MAJOR

NUMBERS, LETTERS AND STARS IN WHITE METAL

THE ARMY

Officers

Commissioned rank is indicated by a more elaborate form of shoulder-strap (also worn by Bandmasters, Music Directors, Administrative officials, Farrier and Fortification First-Class Warrant Officers).

Ranks from Second-Lieutenant to Captain wear shoulder-straps of cords laid alongside each other. *On Field Officers' shoulder-straps it is plaited.*

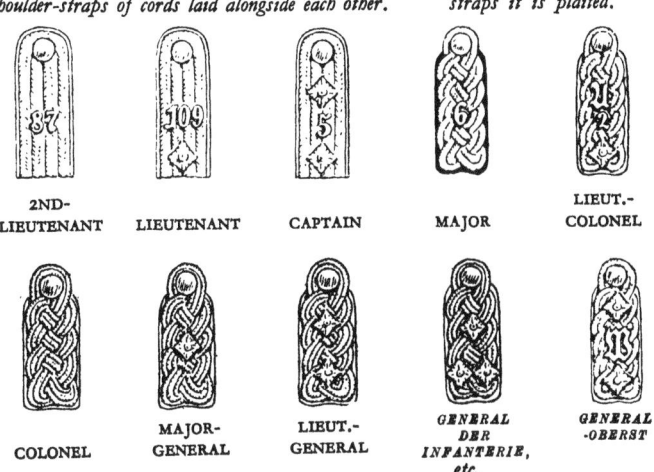

2ND-LIEUTENANT LIEUTENANT CAPTAIN MAJOR LIEUT.-COLONEL

COLONEL MAJOR-GENERAL LIEUT.-GENERAL GENERAL DER INFANTERIE, etc. GENERAL-OBERST

For Officers from the rank of Second-Lieutenant to Colonel the shoulder-straps worn with the Uniform Tunic, White Tunic and Mess Kit—old style (to be described later) are of bright silver cord ; on other uniforms, cord with a matt silver surface is used. All stars, numbers and letters are gilt, the whole being built on a foundation of cloth in *Waffenfarbe*.

On Generals' shoulder-straps the design is in triple cord ; two gold and one silver.

Special regulations relating to Officers' shoulder-straps are as follows :

Officers of the General Staff and Regimental Officers serving with the High Command of the "Wehrmacht" and the Army	No distinguishing badges; Waffenfarbe carmine
Regimental Officers . .	Badges and Waffenfarbe of their unit
Instruction Officers . .	Badges of the school at which they are teaching mounted on the Waffenfarbe of the Service branch from which they come
Officers of Guards Regiments coming from a Jäger Battalion	Badges of Guards Regiment on Waffenfarbe of light green
Other Officers seconded to Staff organizations Commands etc.	Badges on Waffenfarbe of their original unit

The Medical and Veterinary Corps

As might be expected the rod of Æsculapius features prominently on the shoulder-straps of the Medical Corps.

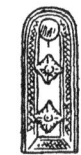    

| APOTHECARY WARRANT OFFICER | MEDICAL WARRANT OFFICER | *Without star :* SURGEON 2ND-LIEUTENANT *One star :* SURGEON LIEUTENANT *Two stars :* SURGEON CAPTAIN | *Without star :* SURGEON CAPTAIN *One star :* SURGEON LIEUT.-COLONEL *Two stars :* SURGEON COLONEL | *Without star :* SURGEON MAJOR-GENERAL *One star :* SURGEON LIEUT.-GENERAL *Two stars :* SURGEON GENERAL |

Surgeon Generals, Veterinary Officers with the rank of General and Medical and Veterinary Warrant Officers show silver stars. Stars for all other ranks are gilt. In all cases the rod and serpent are in the same colour as the stars.

Medical Officers and Warrant Officers of the Military Medical School wear above the Æsculapius emblem a Gothic A.

𝔄

Those attached to the Medical Instruction and Research Section a Gothic L.

𝔏

Medical shoulder-straps are built on a foundation of cornflower-blue, those of the Veterinary Corps on carmine, with the exception of Veterinary and Surgeon Generals whose *Waffenfarbe* is bright red.

VETERINARY WARRANT OFFICER	*Without star:* VETERINARY 2ND-LIEUTENANT *One star:* VETERINARY LIEUTENANT *Two stars:* VETERINARY CAPTAIN	*Without star:* VETERINARY MAJOR *One star:* VETERINARY LIEUT.-COLONEL *Two stars:* VETERINARY COLONEL	*Without star:* VETERINARY MAJOR-GENERAL *One star:* VETERINARY LIEUT.-GENERAL *Two stars:* VETERINARY GENERAL

VETERINARY CORPS BADGE. *A serpent (without rod).*

Regimental Bands

Bandmasters and Music Directors are Honorary Officers of the Army.

BANDMASTER 2ND-LIEUTENANT   BANDMASTER LIEUTENANT   BANDMASTER CAPTAIN   BANDMASTER MAJOR   BANDMASTER LIEUT.-COLONEL

Having no special *Waffenfarbe*, the three junior ranks wear the colour of the service-arm to which their regiment belongs. Bandmaster Majors and Lieutenant-Colonels wear bright red. In addition to their badges of rank they show a lyre in gold.

The design of the shoulder-straps is alternate cords of silver and red for Second-Lieutenants, Lieutenants and Captains ; triple cord (two silver and one red silk,) plaited, for the senior ranks.

Fortification and Farrier Instruction Warrant Officers

Fortifications Warrant Officers wear the uniform of the Engineers, (*Waffenfarbe* black) ; Farrier Instruction Warrant Officers that of the cavalry with the carmine *Waffenfarbe* of the Veterinary Corps. Both wear special shoulder-straps.

THE ARMY

| FORTIFICATIONS WARRANT OFFICER 2ND CLASS | FORTIFICATIONS WARRANT OFFICER 1ST CLASS | FARRIER WARRANT OFFICER INSTRUCTOR 2ND CLASS | FARRIER WARRANT OFFICER INSTRUCTOR 1ST CLASS |

Design woven in black cord with white matt-surfaced artificial silk cord following the shape of the shoulder-strap near the edge. Toothed wheel and star in white metal.

Design woven in yellow wool on a carmine foundation. Horse-shoe and star in white metal.

ORDNANCE OFFICERS

Ordnance Officers wear the shoulder-straps of the Artillery, but instead of the regimental number they show crossed cannon in gilt metal.

RESERVE OFFICERS

The shoulder-straps worn by Officers of the Reserve are constructed on two underlays of different colours, one being the *Waffenfarbe*, the other grey :

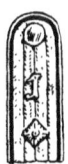 

Service Branch badges (Æsculapius red, serpent, crossed guns, etc.) and regimental badges in gilt.

OFFICER OF THE RESERVE
Medical, Veterinary and Apothecary N.C.O.s in the Reserve do not wear Service branch badges.

Badges (district indicated by Roman numbers in white metal).

OFFICERS OF THE *LANDWEHR*
(Reserves identified with a district.)

Shoulder-straps of "Wehrmachtbeamte"

Although, as in those which have just been described, gold and silver predominate in the shoulder-straps of the *Wehrmachtbeamte*, they have contrived, nevertheless, to introduce the green of their *Waffenfarbe* as well.

It is used to fullest advantage in the shoulder-straps of the Warrant Officers, which are made of dark-green woollen cord with a silver stripe, but it appears quite effectively on those of the commissioned rank officials as well ; a thin strand laid between the plain silver cords of the subaltern, intertwined in the double cords of the major. Generals show it stitched in silk at intervals 1 cm. apart along the plaited two gold and one silver with which the design is worked.

Further distinguishing them from the Army proper are the letters 𝕳 -*Heeresverwaltung* (Army Administration), made up, in the case of officials of the Reserve of non-commissioned rank and those with the rank of General, in white metal ; worn by all others in gilt.

This concludes the indications of rank as shown by arm and shoulder badges.

To be correctly worn, however, they must be accompanied by the proper

THE ARMY

Collar and Cuff Patches

Except by certain Officers in highly specialised branches of the Service, collar patches are not used very much in this country, but, with similar decorations on the cuff, they are a feature of all German uniforms. Incidentally, they provide one of the most easily-noticed of the media used for indicating the *Waffenfarbe*.

For Officers and Men the design is simple:

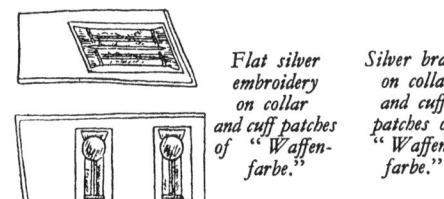
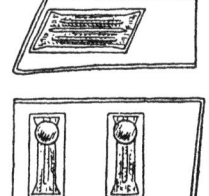

Flat silver embroidery on collar and cuff patches of " Waffenfarbe."

Silver braid on collar and cuff patches of " Waffenfarbe."

N.C.O.s (except those entitled to silver cords on the Uniform Cap) are distinguished by an edging of silver braid on the collar and cuffs of the Uniform Tunic and on the collar of the Field Tunic. Regimental Sergeants-Major wear a double row of braid on the sleeve of both tunics.

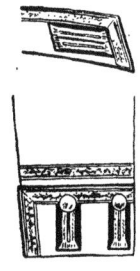

The two upper illustrations show collars of all N.C.O.s (with exceptions noted above). The lower illustrations are of the sleeves of Regimental Sergeants-Major. Other N.C.O.s are similar but have one row of braid only.

UNIFORM TUNIC   FIELD SERVICE TUNIC

The collar and cuff patches of Generals are much
more elaborate, and here is com‑
memorated a feature of uniforms
worn even before the 1815 War
for Freedom.

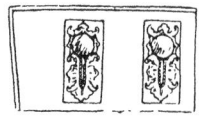

The design, embroidered in gold
on scarlet patches, is that of the
Larisch Infantry Regiment which
was *disbanded* in 1806.

Another design, a little heavier than the ordinary
Officer's but less elaborate than
the General's, is worn by Officers
of the General Staff in silver on
patches of carmine.

For Officers of the High Com‑
mand of the *Wehrmacht* and Army
it is in gold on patches of car‑
mine ; and for Music Directors in gold on scarlet.

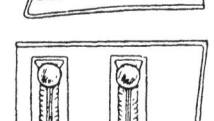

Finally, there are the collar and cuff patches of the
Wehrmachtbeamten. These are divided into four sets :

WEHRMACHTBEAMTEN WITH THE RANK
OF GENERAL

SENIOR *WEHRMACHTBEAMTEN*

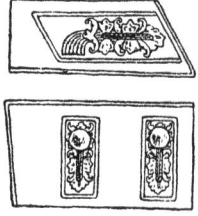
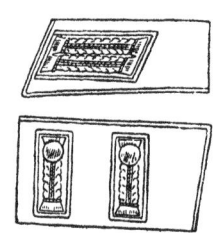

Embroidery bright gold.

Embroidery bright gold on uniform
tunic. Matt‑surfaced gold on field tunic.

THE ARMY

OTHER *WEHRMACHTBEAMTEN* WITH THE RANK OF OFFICER	*WEHRMACHTBEAMTEN* UNDER THE RANK OF OFFICER
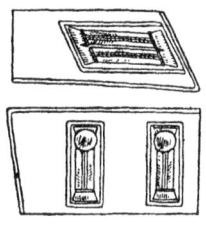	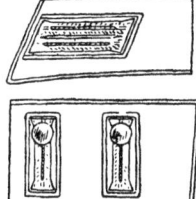
Embroidery for officers attached to the High Command bright gold. Other officials, silver.	*Decoration. Braid woven of silver thread.*

AIGUILLETTES

There are two kinds of *aiguillettes*. These are

the ordinary ones worn by Officers and Administrative Officials with Parade and Full Dress and they are :

    Ordinarily : in silvered cord
 For Music Directors : in silvered cord decorated with red
          silk thread
   For Generals : in gilt cord

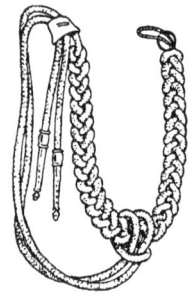

The other type is also of silvered cord but with a dull surface and is worn by Adjutants and Staff Officers.

SHOULDER-STRAPS FOR N.C.O.s AND MEN

The shoulder-straps of N.C.O.s and men differ from those of the Officers in that they are not badges of rank but show only the unit to which the man belongs. As the distinguishing numbers and letters are in *Waffenfarbe* and there is a piping of the same colour, it is easy to recognise the branch of the Service of which the unit forms part.

The shoulder-strap itself is of dark blue-green cloth (except on certain old-style uniforms when it is field grey) and in the case of the Uniform Tunic and Great Coat is sewn on. It is fastened through a loop with a tongue and button on the Field Tunic and Wind Jacket.

An old type of shoulder-strap which is sometimes still worn, instead of being rounded at the top, is cut to a point and has no piping.

Generally speaking, Officers and Men wear the same unit badges, but there are certain cases in which they do not. These are indicated by a * in the examples which follow. Colours mentioned are, of course, the *Waffenfarbe*.

THE ARMY

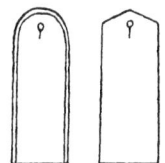

Carmine:
  STAFF-SECTION OF THE ARMY HIGH COMMAND *
Bright Red:
  ORDNANCE DEPARTMENTS *
Black:
  INSPECTION OF EAST AND WEST DEFENCE WORKS *

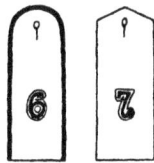

Black (white border):
  ENGINEERS
  RAILWAY ENGINEERS
Cornflower Blue (light-blue border):
  MEDICAL CORPS *

White:
  INFANTRY REGIMENTS
Light Green:
  MOUNTAIN RIFLE REGIMENTS
  (Shoulder-straps broader for numbers greater than 100)

White:
  INFANTRY REGIMENTS
Lemon Yellow:
  SIGNALLING UNITS
Yellow:
  CAVALRY REGIMENTS
Bright Red:
  ARTILLERY REGIMENTS
Rose:
  ARMOURED REGIMENTS — INDEPENDENT ARMOURED SECTIONS
Dark Red:
  SMOKE TROOPS
Light Blue:
  MOTORIZED UNITS
Light Green:
  RIFLE BATTALIONS OF INFANTRY REGIMENTS. MOUNTAIN RIFLE REGIMENTS

White:
  HEADQUARTERS STAFF
  (except XVI Artillery Regt.*)
Yellow:
  DISTRICT REMOUNT SCHOOL
  (with the number of the District)
Orange:
  RECRUITING STAFF *
  (with number of district)
Rose:
  HEADQUARTERS STAFF *
  (XVI Artillery Regt.)
Black:
  FORTRESS INSPECTION STAFF *

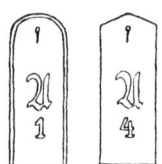

Yellow:
RECONNAISSANCE REGIMENTS
Cornflower Blue (light blue border):
MILITARY SCHOOL OF MEDICINE
(*with number*)

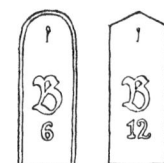

Bright Red:
OBSERVATION SECTIONS

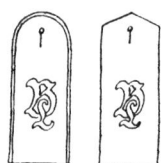

Bright Red:
OBSERVATION INSTRUCTION SECTIONS

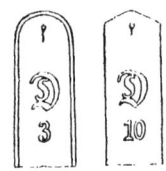

White:
INFANTRY (*Divisional Headquarters Staff**)
Yellow:
LIGHT TROOPS
(*Divisional Headquarters Staff**)
Rose:
ARMOURED TROOPS
(*Divisional Headquarters Staff*)

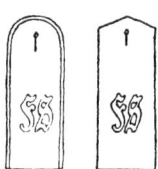

Bright Red:
SCHOOL OF ARTILLERY

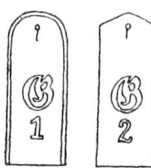

White:
ARMY CORPS HEADQUARTERS STAFF*

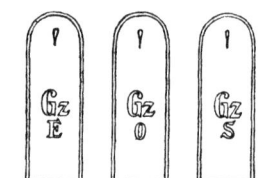

White:
FRONTIER FORCES HEADQUARTERS STAFF
EIFEL, OBERRHEIN, SAARPFALZ

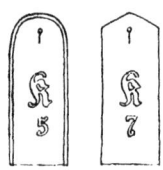

Rose:
MOTOR CYCLE BATTALIONS

White:
STAFF OF MILITARY SCHOOLS
POTSDAM   DRESDEN

1 Senior Official, Air Ministry. Walking-out Dress
2 Major, Veterinary Corps. Walking-out Dress
3 Official, Naval Commissariat. Undress Uniform
4 Army Chaplain. Walking-out Dress
5 Sergeant-Major, Fire-fighting Branch of the Air Force

THE ARMY

White:
STAFF OF MILITARY SCHOOLS
HANOVER   MUNICH

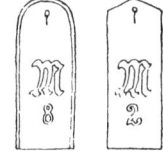

White:
MACHINE-GUN BATTALIONS

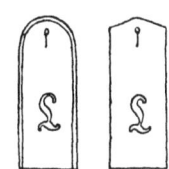

INSTRUCTIONAL UNITS

White:
  INFANTRY
Light Yellow:
  SIGNALS AND RESEARCH
Bright Red:
  ARTILLERY
Rose:
  TANKS
Dark Red:
  SMOKE RESEARCH
Light Blue:
  DRIVER REINFORCEMENTS
  MOTOR-CYCLE REINFORCEMENTS
Cornflower Blue:
  MEDICAL AND MEDICAL RESEARCH

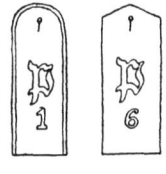

Rose:
ANTI-TANK UNITS

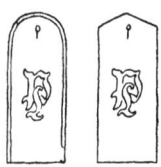

Rose:
ANTI-TANK
INSTRUCTIONAL UNITS

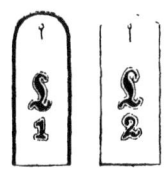

Black:
  ENGINEER INSTRUCTIONAL AND
  RESEARCH BATTALION
  R.U.G.

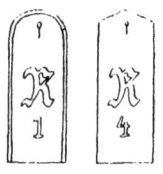

Yellow:
  CYCLE UNIT
Bright Red:
  HORSE ARTILLERY

34   THE ARMY

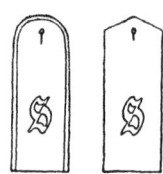

White :
　INFANTRY SCHOOLS
Lemon Yellow :
　SIGNALS SCHOOLS
Yellow :
　CAVALRY SCHOOLS
Bright Red :
　ARTILLERY SCHOOLS
Rose :
　SCHOOLS FOR ARMOURED TROOPS
Dark Red :
　ANTI-GAS SCHOOLS
Light Blue :
　HORSE TRANSPORT SCHOOLS

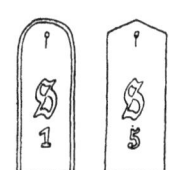

Yellow :
　DISMOUNTED CAVALRY REGIMENTS
Rose :
　RIFLE REGIMENTS
Black (white border) :
　ENGINEER SCHOOLS

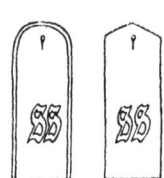

White :
　ARMY PHYSICAL CULTURE SCHOOLS

White :
　SCHOOLS FOR N.C.O.S
　　　　POTSDAM

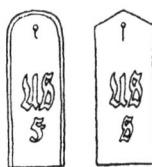

White :
　　　　SCHOOL FOR N.C.O.S
　FRANKENSTEIN　　　SIGMARINGEN

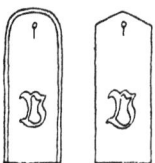

Rose :
　TANK RESEARCH SECTION

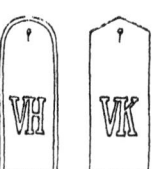

Bright Red :
　　　EXPERIMENTAL STATIONS
　HILLERSLEBEN　　　KUMMERSDORF

THE ARMY

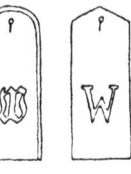 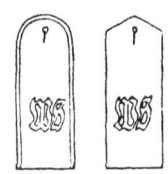

White:
GUARDS GUARDS
REGIMENTS BATTALIONS
BERLIN VIENNA

Bright Red:
ORDNANCE SCHOOL

The Modern Uniform

A casual observer, visiting Germany to-day after an absence of, say, twenty-five years, would find very little change in the uniform of the Army. Two great political upheavals have taken place during that time, each of them to be the creator of a new order and a new tradition. Be that as it may, they both appear to have considered it unnecessary (or perhaps unwise) to make any startling changes in the established order of the Fighting Forces—at any rate so far as is outwardly visible. The incorporation of the swastika in all badges featuring the national eagle is, of course, a somewhat drastic innovation, and changes in internal administration and methods of warfare have inevitably brought about certain alterations and additions, but, broadly speaking, the German soldier in his field-grey uniform, some of its features dating from the Prussian war with Napoleon, looks much the same as he did during the World War of 1914–18.

Types of Uniform

The German Army is dressed after the method universally adopted. That is to say, with the exception of certain specialists who are dressed with an eye to the exigencies of the work they do, all Men, N.C.O.s and Officers wear a basic uniform, the various ranks being denoted by badges. It sounds simple enough, but when one remembers how irresistibly attracted his countrymen are to the decorative aspect of the military game, one is not, perhaps, surprised to learn of the variety of uses to which the German soldier manages to put his wardrobe.

He has a :

Field Dress	Undress Uniform	Mess Kit (*only for Officers*)
Service Dress	(*only for Officers and Warrant Officers*)	
Guard Uniform		Full Dress Kit (*only for Officers*)
Parade Uniform	Reporting Uniform	
		Walking-Out Dress
		Sports Kit

And now let us deal with the various uniforms in greater detail.

One might start with the headgear, since, perhaps, one of the most characteristic features of the German uniform is :

The Steel Helmet

Field-grey in colour, like the uniform with which it is worn, it looks like this :

THE ARMY

SEEN FROM RIGHT   WEHRMACHT EAGLE   SEEN FROM LEFT

The shield on the right side is barred in the national colours (black, white and red), and the *Wehrmacht* eagle (which, as distinct from the more usual type of National Emblem, it will be noticed has folded wings) is in silver-grey on a black background. The chin-strap is black.

For use in battle practice where there are two opposing sides, a band is supplied, coloured red

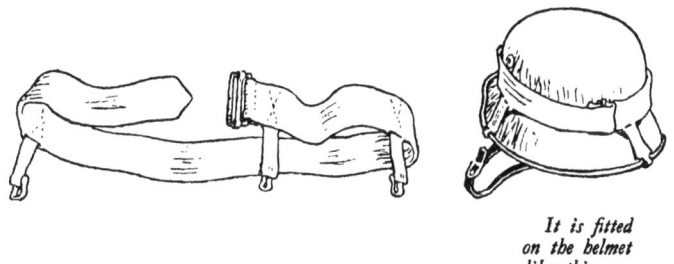

It is fitted on the helmet like this

on one side and yellow on the other. It can be worn with either the red or the yellow side uppermost.

The Steel Helmet is worn with Field Dress, Parade Dress and Guard Uniform.

It is true that one is inclined to associate the German soldier with his Steel Helmet, but, fortunately for him, he is not expected to wear it all the time and so when something less cumbersome is called for he substitutes

The Uniform Cap

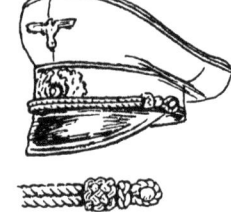

THE UNIFORM CAP
FOR N.C.O.S FOR OFFICERS

Here again the ground colour is field-grey, but a contrast is provided by a cap-band of dark blue-green and a black leather peak.

Superficially, the cap is the same for Officers and Men, but there is one main difference. In the case of the ranks (with the exception of certain specialist N.C.O.s), the chin-strap matches the peak, but Officers below the rank of Major-General—and that applies also to Administrative Officials—wear instead two silver cords (Generals, gilt cords), a distinction made also in the case of the exceptions mentioned above which include Ensigns, Veterinary, Medical, Apothecary, Artillery and Paymaster Warrant Officers.

You will remember my mentioning earlier that there are very few articles of uniform on which the distinguishing colours of the various branches of the service do not appear somewhere or other. On

THE ARMY

the uniform cap it is used as a piping for all ranks except Generals, whose caps are piped with gold to match their cords.

The illustrations above show how the two standard badges are worn—the Emblem above the Cockade—but sometimes it will be noticed that a third badge has been inserted between the two. This is a memorial badge worn in memory of the great traditions of certain regiments when, previous to 1918, they had a separate identity.

Below are three examples:

DEATH'S HEAD
In matt-surfaced white metal commemorating the 1st and 2nd Regiments of Prussian Life Guards: worn by 1st Squadron 5th Cavalry Regiment.

DRAGOON EAGLE
In matt-surfaced gilt metal commemorating the 5th Brandenburg Dragoon Regiment. Worn by regimental staff of second and fourth squadron of the 6th Cavalry. Regiments and 3rd Motor Cyclist Battalion.

DEATH'S HEAD
In matt-surfaced white metal commemorating the Brunswick 92nd Infantry Regiment and the 17th Regiment of Hussars. Worn by the regimental staff of the 1st and 2nd Battalions and the 13th Company of the 17th Infantry Regiment and the 2nd Squadron of the 15th Cavalry Regiment.

Mounted, this is how they look:

FOR N.C.O.S AND MEN OF THE 5TH BATTALION 1ST CAVALRY REGIMENT

The Uniform Peaked Cap is worn :

With Service Dress and Undress uniform, by Officers and N.C.O.s.
With Parade Dress, by Officers when not actually on duty.
With Walking-Out Dress and with Dress uniforms by Officers.

THE FIELD SERVICE CAP

But there are contingencies which, it is considered, have still to be provided for, so there is also the Field Service Cap, described officially as being " for use on occasions other than those prescribed for the Steel Helmet and Uniform Cap ". It is worn by Men, N.C.O.s and Officers up to the rank of Colonel. Generals please themselves.

The cap worn by Men and N.C.O.s is of simple design, ornamented only with the National Emblem worked in silver-grey cotton yarn, the Cockade, and a sort of inverted Lance-Corporal's stripe in *Waffenfarbe* to indicate the wearer's Branch of the Service.

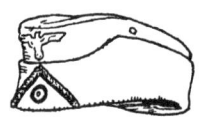

For Officers, Warrant Officers entitled to silver cords (see first paragraph on Uniform Cap) and Administrative Officials with Officer's rank, there are two types of Field Service Cap :

THE ARMY

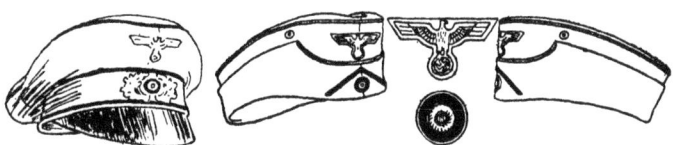

THE OLD STYLE
which may be worn until April 1942.

THE NEW STYLE
which dates from June 6th, 1938

The old model resembles the Uniform Peaked Cap except that the badges are less elaborate and the peak is of soft leather. The new type, however, it will be seen, follows closely the cut of the Field Cap for N.C.O.s and Men.

Badges and material are, of course, of better quality, and the crown, the front of the turn-up and the cockade are piped with an aluminium cord, but otherwise the design is the same.

THE MOUNTAIN CAP

Finally, there is the Mountain Cap; field-grey in summer, covered with white cloth in winter; badges as on the Field Service Cap.

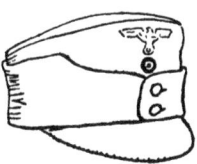

It is worn principally by mountain regiments, replacing the steel helmet and field cap, but other troops use it for ski-ing, either on or off duty.

The Uniform Tunic

Worn by all ranks, this forms part of what one might call the German soldier's number one uniform. It is the tunic he wears when he is on parade, walking out, and for all ceremonial occasions.

Front View.   *Rear View.*
THIS SHOWS THE UNIFORM AS WORN BY N.C.O.S AND MEN

It is of the inevitable field-grey, with collar and cuffs of dark blue-green and white-metal buttons (gilt for Generals). *Waffenfarbe* is used for piping round the base of the collar, on the upper edges of the cuff, outlining the collar and cuff patches, the shoulder-straps (N.C.O.s and Men), the back pockets and down the tunic overlap in front.

The National Emblem has two forms:

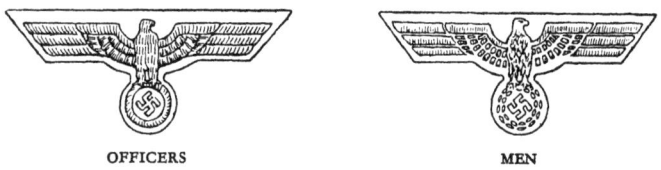

OFFICERS   MEN

THE ARMY 43

For Officers it is embroidered on what is called badge-cloth—the dark blue-green material of the collar and cuffs—and sewn on the tunic. On the Men's tunic it is a white-metal badge clipped on. N.C.O.s who buy their own tunics, however, may use the embroidered eagle.

THE FIELD SERVICE TUNIC (MEN AND N.C.O.s)

Lighter and more suitable for work is the Field Service Tunic, also of field-grey, with collar, collar patches and shoulder-straps of dark blue-green badge-cloth. The buttons are matt-surfaced grey. The National Emblem is carried out in silver-grey cotton yarn.

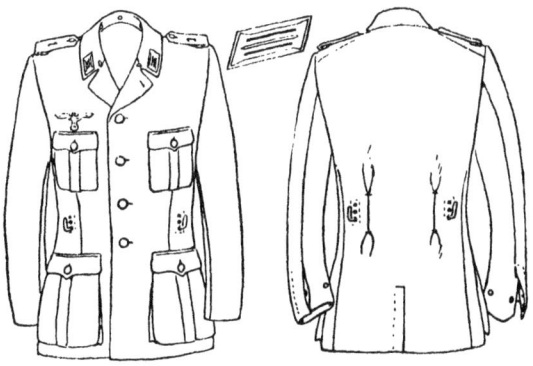

FIELD SERVICE TUNIC OF N.C.O.S AND MEN

Generally, for N.C.O.s and men, the collar of the Field Service Tunic is worn closed, but in suitable weather, and if it is convenient for the work they are doing, it may be worn open. Permission to undo a button or two on a long route march used to be a concession much appreciated. In future it is to be encouraged.

The belt supports, back and front, can be removed when they are not required (when the Field Service Tunic is used as a Walking-Out Uniform, for example), and buttons clipped on in place of them.

The Field Service Tunic for Officers

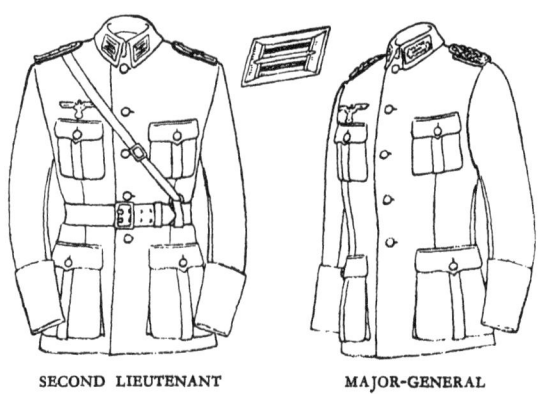

SECOND LIEUTENANT   MAJOR-GENERAL

This is also usually worn closed, but in the country the collar and top button may be unfastened. The National Emblem is embroidered in silver thread.

On the Field Service Tunic for Officers, badges, etc., are less elaborate than on the Uniform Tunic. But in the case of Generals and the highest Administrative Officials there is no difference.

THE ARMY

The Field Tunic IS worn as	The Field Tunic MAY be worn as
Field Dress Service Dress	Undress Uniform Informal Mess Dress for Officers Walking-Out Dress for Officers

THE PIPED FIELD SERVICE TUNIC

A compromise between the two uniforms just described is the Piped Field Service Tunic.

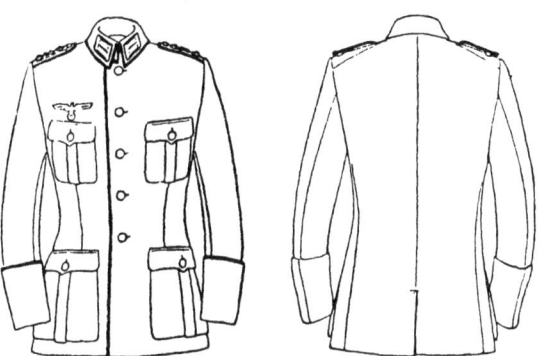

It is the utilitarian Field Service Tunic with some of the brighter features of the Uniform Tunic—piping in *Waffenfarbe* down the front overlap of the coat, on the cuffs and round the collar; shoulder-straps, collar patches, emblem and buttons as on the Uniform Tunic. Its use, however, is restricted to Officers, Ensigns, *Wehrmachtbeamten* and those entitled to wear the Officer's Uniform Cap.

Old Style Tunics

Dating from pre-Nazi days there are still a few old uniforms to be seen.

(1) The tunic of the *Reichsheer* (the Army of 100,000 allowed to Germany by the Treaty of Versailles), used as Field Dress by Officers and Men, non-issue Walking-Out Dress for N.C.O.s and Men, and Dress Uniform for Officers.

(2) Tunics made over from the Uniforms of the former Austrian Army.

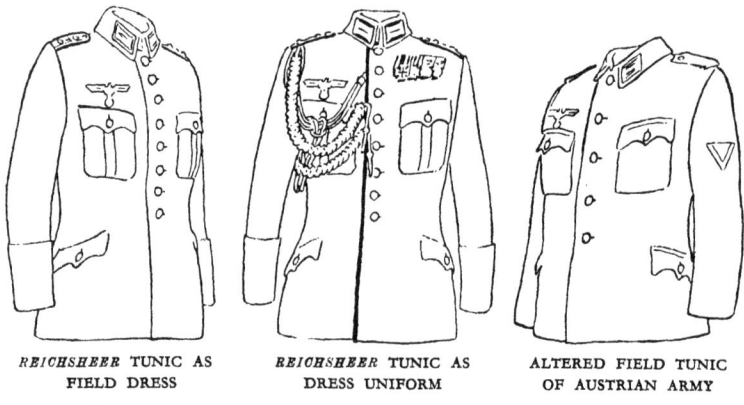

REICHSHEER TUNIC AS FIELD DRESS   REICHSHEER TUNIC AS DRESS UNIFORM   ALTERED FIELD TUNIC OF AUSTRIAN ARMY

These tunics may be freely worn (except on Parade). No orders have yet been issued ordering their withdrawal.

The White Tunic for Officers and "Wehrmachtbeamten" with Officer's Rank

A White Tunic is included in the wardrobe of Officers for use in barracks or for riding. It is not

THE ARMY

usually worn on duty except when the troops are in P.T. kit.

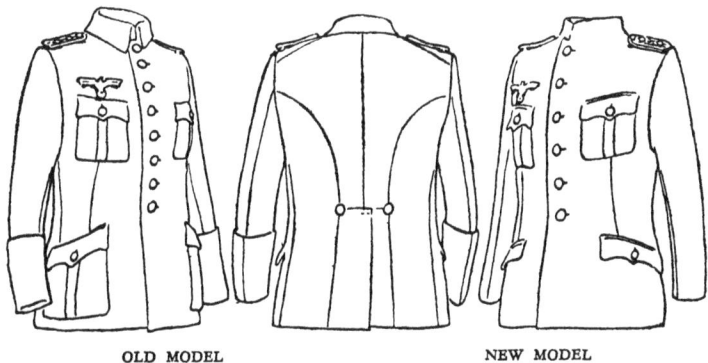

OLD MODEL   NEW MODEL

Badges and shoulder-straps are worn as with the Uniform Tunic; the National Emblem in white-metal is mounted on a pin (for Generals in gilt).

Special Uniforms of the Mechanized Fighting Troops

For troops serving with armoured cars, tanks, etc., there is a special uniform of black cloth; Beret, Field Jacket and Trousers fastened round the ankle.

The Beret

shows inevitably the National Emblem (N.C.O.s and Men in silver-grey cotton yarn; Officers in silver thread)

The Field Jacket (colour, black)

is piped in *Waffenfarbe* round the shoulder-straps, collar and cuff patches—the last-named showing a Death's Head in aluminium. Officers' shoulder-straps are the same as with the Field Tunic and the National Emblem worn on the right breast is, for all ranks, of silver-grey cotton yarn on a black underlay.

The Trousers

Black without piping.

Frogs are worn with this uniform but no side-arms. On parade, Officers wear belts and aiguillettes; Men, marksmanship lanyards.

Footwear

Light lacing shoes.

OVERALLS

For fatigue duties in barracks, N.C.O.s and Men have two-piece field-grey overalls.

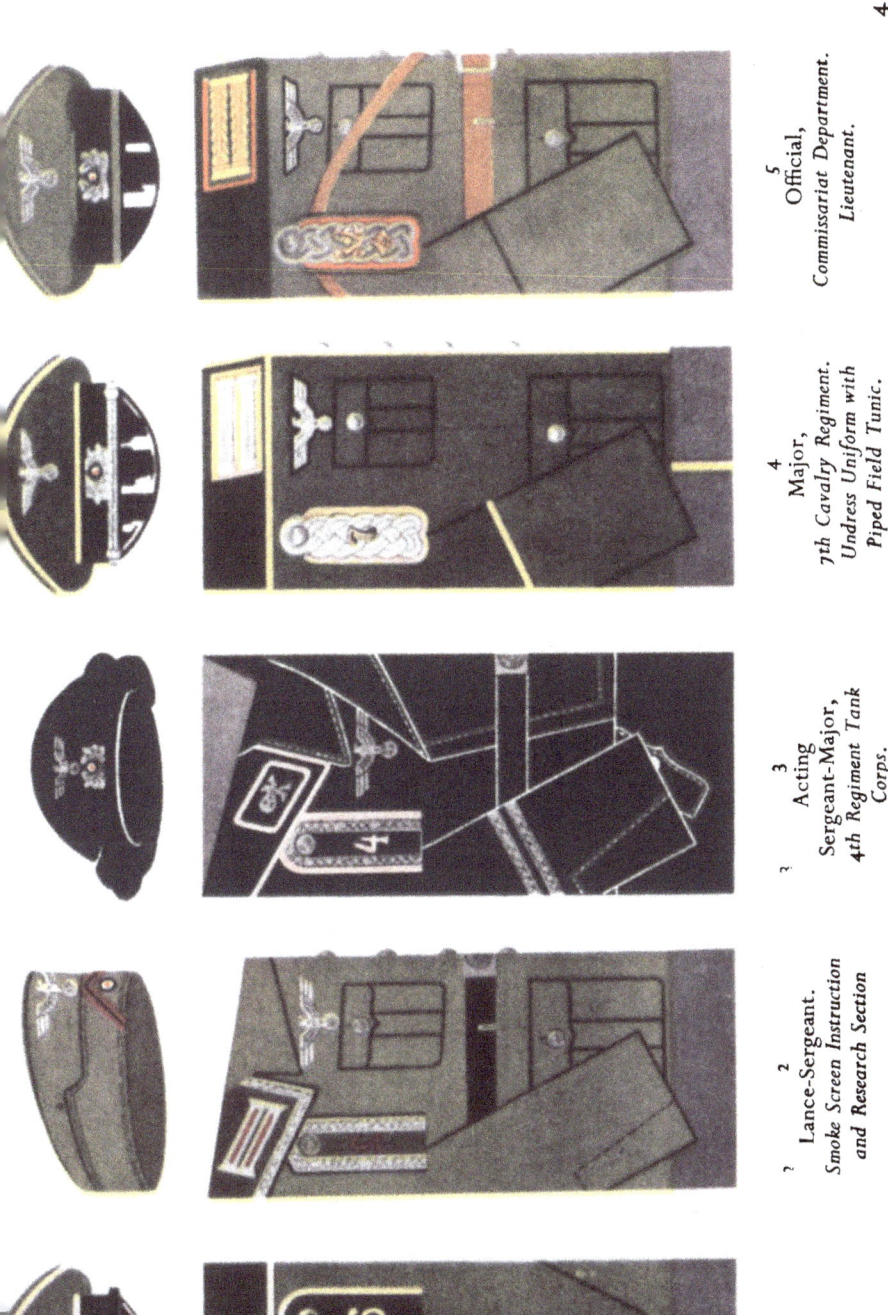

1. Private, 6th Regiment. Tank Corps
2. Lance-Sergeant. Smoke Screen Instruction and Research Section
3. Acting Sergeant-Major, 4th Regiment Tank Corps.
4. Major, 7th Cavalry Regiment. Undress Uniform with Piped Field Tunic.
5. Official, Commissariat Department. Lieutenant.

THE ARMY

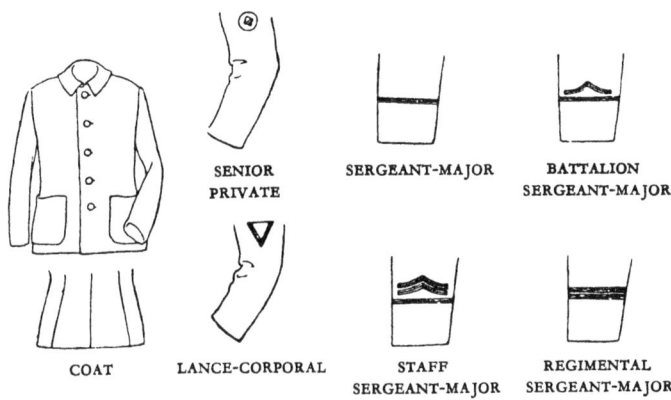

The Great-Coat

As worn by Officers (except Generals) N.C.O.s and Men.

Colour . .	Field-grey with dark blue-green collar. Grey buttons
For N.C.O.s and Men	Shoulder-straps piped in *Waffenfarbe* as on Uniform Tunic
For Officers to the rank of Colonel	Shoulder-straps as on Field Service Tunic
For Generals .	The top two buttons are left undone showing bright red lapels. Buttons, gilt

Cloaks

For informal occasions, Officers and Administrative Officials with Officers' rank have a cloak of field-grey with a dark blue-green collar.

Wind Jackets and Waterproofs for Mountain Troops

Made up in olive-green calico with shoulder-straps

THE ARMY

but no other badges it is loose enough to be worn over a cartridge belt.

Waterproofs in field-grey are issued to Motor-Cyclists. They are worn with clipped-on shoulder-straps.

SERVICE DRESS OF ARMY CHAPLAINS

Violet is the predominant colour-note in the dress of German Army clericals.

Officers without definite rank, they are classed as Chaplains, and in their more senior grade, as Field Bishops.

When accompanying troops in the field they wear a special form of Field Service Tunic, grey with violet collar patches, and silver embroidery; a belt with shoulder-strap, Officer's trousers with a violet piping and Officer's boots.

Field Bishops have gold instead of silver embroidery.

The Cap worn by the ordinary Chaplain also has violet piping, to which are added two gold pipings in the case of Field Bishops, who also wear the gilt cord chin-strap peculiar to Generals. Between the National Emblem and the cockade on the front of the cap is a Gothic cross. Chaplains wear these cap emblems, the emblem on their tunic and the buttons, in the materials prescribed for officers. Field Bishops, however, wear a gold emblem on their tunics.

On occasions other than field service, Chaplains and Field Bishops wear a Frock-Coat with white-metal and matt gilt buttons respectively.

It is a field-grey coat with violet collar and piping and has the National Emblem as worn by Officers.

The overcoat has no epaulettes and matt grey buttons, except for the Field Bishop, who has gilt buttons and violet lapels.

On special occasions a gold cross is worn on the breast.

Trousers of all Branches

A rather lighter shade of grey, without any tinge of the green shown in the field-grey of the tunics, is used for all trousers.

As with the Uniform Tunic and Field Service Tunic, pipings of the appropriate *Waffenfarbe* are worn on slacks. On the infantry breeches and the riding breeches of mounted troops, however, they are not used, except in the case of Generals and staff Officers.

Generals and Officials of equivalent rank have a broad red stripe down the side seams of both breeches and slacks. General Staff and Regimental Officers attached to the High Command have a broad carmine stripe, with a double piping of braid upon it.

In Field Dress proper no pipings of any kind are worn, the same being true in the case of the " mountain " trousers issued to the *Gebirgs-Jäger*-Regiments and similar trousers of black cloth worn by Officers and Men of the Tank and Armoured units. In both cases these are a form of ski-ing trouser fastened round the ankle.

Officers' slacks may have straps under the instep, the same applying to walking-out uniforms, privately made and worn by many N.C.O.s and Men.

White trousers, for wear off duty in summer, are issued to all ranks.

Boots

In the Infantry and similar troops, all N.C.O.s and Men wear three-quarter length marching-boots. These have no laces and are of black leather. They are worn with slacks for all field-service, in Guard Uniform and for parade purposes. The shorter lacing ankle boots are for walking out and for use with slacks in some forms of Full Dress.

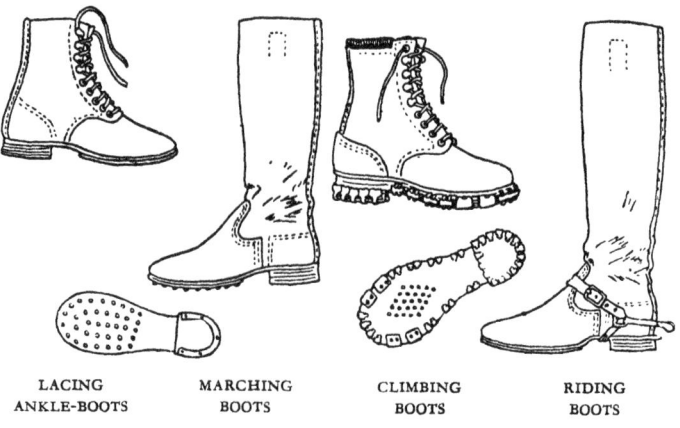

| LACING ANKLE-BOOTS | MARCHING BOOTS | CLIMBING BOOTS | RIDING BOOTS |

As will be seen in the accompanying drawing, climbing boots, suitably nailed round the edges of the soles, are issued to mountain troops, for use with the mountain trousers mentioned above.

Officers of all Arms wear riding boots, with breeches, as do the other ranks in mounted units. Spurs are worn by mounted troops, but may also be worn by Infantry Officers in Parade Dress, etc., and by Staff Officers. Black laced ankle boots are worn

THE ARMY 55

with slacks, but half-wellingtons may only be worn with " overalls " strapped beneath the instep.

Warrant Officers who are responsible for their own uniforms have the footwear of Officers.

On all parades and on field service, regulation footwear is obligatory; off-duty, any form of black boot is allowable both for commissioned and other ranks, but authority frowns upon the wearing of shoes or of button-boots.

Specialist Badges

Specialist badges are worn on the right lower arm of Uniform Tunics, Field Tunics and Great-Coats. Worked in yellow wool on dark blue-green cloth, they are as follows :

MEDICAL PERSONNEL
(*end of 1st year Medical School*)

FARRIER N.C.O.S
(*qualified*)

ORDNANCE N.C.O.S
(*qualified*)

ARTILLERY SERGEANTS-MAJOR

SADDLERS

RADIO N.C.O.S

PIGEON POSTMASTERS

FORTRESS ENGINEER-SERGEANTS-MAJOR

FORTIFICATION
SERGEANTS-MAJOR

PAYMASTER
N.C.O.S

REGIMENTAL SADDLER
N.C.O.S

DEFENCE WORKS
SERGEANTS-MAJOR

These two badges, however, are worn above the rank badge on the left arm :

OFFICERS AND MEN OF THE ENGINEERS WHO HAVE PASSED MILITARY DRIVING TEST FOR MOTOR-BOATS ON INLAND WATERS. (*Anchor in silver embroidery.*)

OFFICERS AND MEN OF ALL SIGNAL SECTIONS OTHER THAN THE CORPS OF SIGNALS. (*Flash in " Waffenfarben."*)

and these two on the left lower arm :

GUN-LAYERS' BADGE
ARTILLERY
(*yellow matt silk*)

OPERATORS' BADGE
SMOKE TROOPS
(*white matt silk*)

The Marksman's Lanyard

The Lanyard is awarded for skill in marksmanship and, for every time it is won, a decoration is added to it as follows:

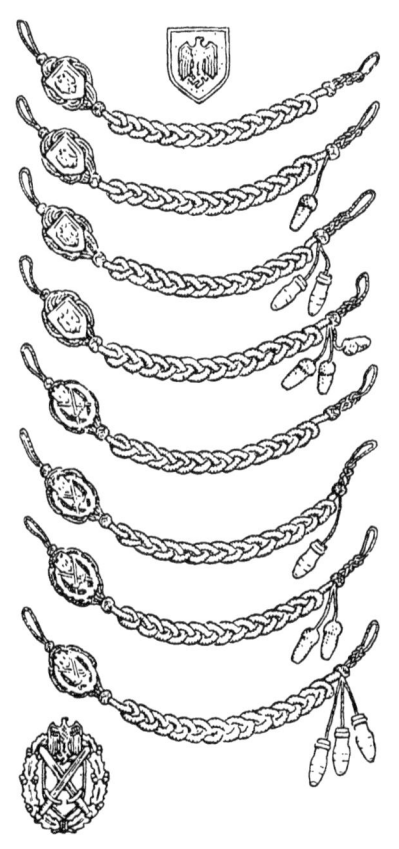

Awards
1- 4. A white-metal shield showing the national emblem, an acorn being added for every successive award.

5- 8. A white-metal shield with crossed swords and a wreath of oak-leaves, an acorn being added for every successive award.

9-12. A shield as for 5-8 but in gilt, with an acorn for every successive award.
(Artillery Regiments use miniature grenades instead of acorns.)

Recently, new badges have been designed and will

gradually replace the shields shown above. Here they are:

1ST–4TH AWARD	1ST–4TH AWARD	ARMOURED TROOPS 5TH–9TH AWARD	9TH–12TH AWARD
(*matt aluminium*)	(*matt aluminium*)	(*matt aluminium*)	(*matt gilt*)

The Lanyard of matt silvered cord, is worn from the right shoulder to the second tunic button, with Parade, Walking-Out and Guard uniforms.

Standard Bearers

Standard Bearers wear on the right upper-arm a badge made of crossed flags in their Regimental Colours, the *Wehrmacht* eagle and an oak leaf.

"Swallows Nests"

The sign of a Bandsman or a Bugler is what the Germans call a "Swallows Nest" on each shoulder.

THE ARMY

They are of *Waffenfarbe* trimmed in the case of:

Drum and Fife bands: with a field-grey border.
Regimental Bandsmen and Trumpeters: with bright silver braid.
Buglers: as for Bandsmen, with, in addition, a 7-cm. long silver fringe.

MOUNTAIN GUIDES BADGE

N.C.O.s and Men who are recognized guides wear a special badge on the left breast. On the Uniform Tunic its lower edge should be on a level with the third button counting from below; on the Field Service Tunic it is sewn on the breast pocket. The badge is a white enamelled Edelweiss with a gold centre, on a green ground; on a white border is the word *Heeresbergführer* (Army Mountain Guide).

FAUSTRIEMEN AND TRODDELN (*side-arm Tassels*)

Perhaps the most traditionally interesting feature of the modern German uniform is the side-arm tassel. It has two forms, one the *Troddel*, worn by Foot Regiments, and the *Faustriemen*, worn by Cavalry Regiments.

They are not purely decorative, as one might suppose; they can, on the contrary, be extremely informative to those who know how to read them. But, although they show with the greatest precision the exact whereabouts of the wearer in his regiment, the method used is as complicated as it is ingenious and I would suggest that, if you want to know to which company of what battalion a man belongs, you would save time and probably arrive at the information more accurately, if you ask him rather than try to get it from his side-arm tassel.

However, it is interesting to know how it is done, so here is the system.

Take the case of a regiment of five Battalions and twenty Companies, the Companies being numbered consecutively from first to last. The colours are apportioned thus:

Dark Green	Headquarters
White	1st Battalion
Red	2nd ,,
Yellow	3rd ,,
Cornflower Blue	4th ,,
Light Green	5th ,,

THE ARMY

Strap and Tassel.	Stock of "Troddel". Top of "Faustriemen".	Top and Crown of "Troddel". Crown of "Faustriemen".	Battalions and "Abteilungen".	Companies.	Squadrons.	Batteries.
Dark Green	Dark Green	Dark Green	Headquarters	—	—	—
,,	,,	White	—	13	—	—
,,	,,	Red	—	14	—	—
Field-Grey	,,	White	—	S	—	S
Dark Green	White	Dark Green	I	—	—	†
Field-Grey	,,	White	—	1	1	1
,,	,,	Red	—	2	2	2
,,	,,	Yellow	—	3	3	3
,,	,,	Cornflower Blue	—	4	4	—
Dark Green	Red	Light Green	—	—	5	—
Field-Grey	,,	Dark Green	II	—	—	—
,,	,,	White	—	5	6	4
,,	,,	Red	—	6	7	5
,,	,,	Yellow	—	7	8	6
,,	,,	Cornflower Blue	—	8	9	—
Dark Green	Yellow	Light Green	—	—	10	—
Field-Grey	,,	Dark Green	III	—	—	—
,,	,,	White	—	9	11	7
,,	,,	Red	—	10	—	8
,,	,,	Yellow	—	11	—	9
,,	,,	Cornflower Blue	—	12	—	—
Dark Green	Cornflower Blue	Dark Green	IV	—	—	—
Field-Grey	,,	White	—	15	—	—
,,	,,	Red	—	16	—	—
,,	,,	Yellow	—	17	—	—
Dark Green	Light Green	Dark Green	V	—	—	—
Field-Grey	,,	White	—	18	—	—
,,	,,	Red	—	19	—	—
,,	,,	Yellow	—	20	—	—

* In the German Army, Cavalry Regiments are divided into three *Abteilungen* and eleven Squadrons; Artillery Regiments into three *Abteilungen*, nine Batteries and a Supplementary Battery. † Supplementary.

Now the *Troddel* is divided in this way :

(a) The Strap is coloured dark green for the Staff and the 13th and 14th Company; grey for the others.
(b) The Top is in the Company colour (see table on next page).
(c) The Stock is in the Battalion colour.
(d) The Crown like the top is in the Company colour.
(e) The Tassel green or grey to match the strap.

The *Faustriemen* is similarly divided :

(a) The Leather Strap is Field-Grey.
(b) The Top is in the *Abteilung* colour.
(c) The Crown is in the Squadron colour.
(d) The Tassel is dark green for Staff and light grey for the Squadrons.

The system is the same for Infantry and Artillery regiments, but as the number of Companies, Squadrons or Battalions differs according to the Arm of the Service to which the regiment belongs, the *Troddeln* are not constant in their colouring. For example (referring to the table on the previous page) the 8th Company of an Infantry Regiment being the 4th Company of the 2nd Battalion the *Troddel* has a cornflower blue Top and Crown and a red Stock ; but the 8th Battery of an Artillery Regiment is the 2nd Battery of the 3rd Abteilung and therefore has a red Top and Crown and a yellow Stock.

N.C.O.s

Cadet Corporals, Lance-Sergeants and Sergeants wear *Troddeln* and *Faustriemen* of a special design without relation to their Company colours :

THE ARMY

STRAP: *Dark Green with 3 silver stripes on each side.*

STOCK, TOP AND CROWN: *Dark Green with silver thread decoration.*

TASSEL: *Silver (matt surfaced).*

STRAP: *Light Grey.*
TOP: *Field-Grey.*

CROWN: *Dark Green with silver decoration.*

TASSEL: *Silver (matt surfaced).*

N.C.O.s and Men of the 3rd Battalion of the 67th Infantry Regiment wear, to commemorate the 1st Prussian Grenadier Guards, their *Troddeln* on a strap of red Russia leather.

Side-Arms

Every foot-soldier from Private to Ensign wears, slung on his regulation belt, a frog, also of black leather, for carrying his bayonet. He wears his bayonet with all uniforms, fixing on it as soon as it is in place, his *Troddel* or *Portepee*.

The cavalryman, on the other hand, has various regulations for the carrying of side-arms. For example, when mounted and in Service or Field Dress, he wears his bayonet only when he has his rifle, carrying it in addition to a sabre at his saddle. Then, with Parade Dress the rule is sabre only, but with Guard Uniform and for duty when not mounted, only the bayonet is worn.

You will remember that cavalrymen wear, instead of the *Troddel*, *Faustriemen*. There is no difference between them in so far as concerns the way they are worn but it sometimes happens, as explained above, that an occasion will arise when two different side-arms are worn at the same time. One does not, however, as might be supposed, wear two *Faustriemen*. The rule is that only one may be used, attached in the case of sabre and bayonet, to the former.

There is no special bayonet or belt issued to warrant officers, but they are entitled to wear an Officer's sabre and on certain occasions may substitute an automatic pistol for the usual side-arms. Senior Ensigns, however, along with medical, apothecary and veterinary W.O.s and certain grades of Artillery and Paymaster Warrant Officers have a right to the Officer's belt which is of brown leather and can, if they like, wear an Officer's dirk when they walk out.

Below are a few illustrations of side-arms fittings showing the method of attaching *Troddeln*, *Portepees*, etc.

BUCKLE IN METAL LACQUERED GREY

BELT WITH BUCKLE AND SIDE-ARM FROG

OFFICER'S BROWN LEATHER BELT WITH SHOULDER-STRAP

THE ARMY

  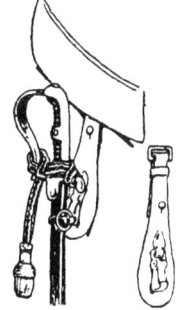

| SIDE-ARM FROG (CAVALRY MODEL NOW USED FOR INFANTRY ALSO) | BELT WITH ATTACHMENT FOR MEN'S SABRE | ATTACHMENT FOR SUSPENDING SABRE OUTSIDE GREAT COAT |

Portepees

In place of *Troddeln* and *Faustriemen* all ranks from Ensigns upwards wear *Portepees*. They are somewhat similar but are worn:

With sabre and bayonet on field-grey leather straps decorated with 4 silver stripes.   *With dirk; on silver cords.*

The Stock, Crown and Tassel of both *Portepees* are of cord bound with silver wire.

Officers

Side-arms for Officers are the same as for Men, i.e. bayonet and sabre, but they also have the right, which, as has already been mentioned, they share with certain N.C.O.s, to wear a dirk and on occasions an automatic. All that has been said in this section applies as usual to Administrative Officials.

PART II
THE NAVY

THE NAVY

IN THE YEAR 1848, the Prussian Navy came into being under Friedrich-William IV. To-day the Officers and Men of the Navy of Adolf Hitler's Germany wear practically the same blue uniform as their forefathers did nearly a hundred years ago.

Naturally, it bears little resemblance to the uniform of the other two Services (except perhaps for the Officers' shoulder-straps which are much the same for all three Arms of the *Wehrmacht*), but lately, certain units which are mostly employed on work ashore, have been put into a field-grey rig which is difficult to distinguish from the uniform of the Army. In fact, except for the oak-leaves in gold on the uniform cap and the embossed anchor on the buttons, it is almost identical.

But to return to the blue uniform. The idea, used in the Army, of a basic uniform to be worn by all ranks, with Officers, N.C.O.s and Men distinguishable from each other only by badges, does not obtain in the Navy. They use instead the method we ourselves have adopted. Petty Officers and Men have a uniform of their own; Warrant Officers are dressed to some extent like Commissioned Officers but with differences which make their standing easily recognizable.

All ratings wear a badge indicating the branch of the Service to which they belong, i.e. Executive, Engineers, Ordnance, etc.

Organization of the Navy

Generally speaking, the various ratings of the Navy have their equivalents in the ranks of the Army, and as in the Army, these ratings are identified with the departments to which they belong. In other words, in the Navy there is the equivalent of a Private, Lance-Corporal, Sergeant, etc., in the following branches :

Deck (boatswains, etc.)	Administrative Ratings
Engine Room	Writers
Signallers	Medical Ratings
Telegraphists	Bandsmen
Carpenters	Marine Artillery (Land)
Artificers	Aircraft spotters

Cadets and Midshipmen

The system of training Officers is the same as in the other Services. That is to say, before an Officer is commissioned, he must start at the bottom and work his way up.

Like our own Special Entry candidates, the first step is an entrance examination but from there on the resemblance ceases. They start in immediately on a period of five and a half months' intensive training—the first ten weeks of it are spent drilling on the barrack square. Then follows a period at sea, but only on probation for three months. Those who give a satisfactory account of themselves are given the rank of cadet and the privilege of serving as a lower-deck rating. For ten months they live the life of an ordinary seaman, then comes another examination, the cadet is promoted to midshipman and goes off to a Naval Training Establishment for two years. He now rates as Petty Officer. When he passes out and goes to sea, however, he may become a Warrant Officer but a Warrant Officer he remains until he is elected a sub-Lieutenant by the Officers of his ship.

Active Officers

The Active Officers of the Navy are divided into seven main branches or *Laufbahnen* as they are called in German :

Executive Officers.
Engineer Officers.
Gunnery Officers.
Medical Officers.
Ordnance Officers, subdivided into Officers of Offensive and Defensive Ordnance.
Administration Officers (not to be confused with Administrative Officials).
Signal Officers.

Reserve Officers

As in the Army, the Navy has a Reserve, a " *zur Verfügung* " and a *zur Disposition* List (see section on the Organization of the Army).

Musicians

Bandmasters and Music Directors wear Officer's uniform but their rank is honorary.

Marinebeamten

For those who are particularly interested in the Navy and who possibly tackle this part of the book first, perhaps it would be advisable to repeat the explanation which has already been given in the Army section relating to Administrative Officials.

In all three branches of the *Wehrmacht*, certain Officials who are employed in the various Ministries, Government Departments, etc., on administrative work in connection with the Services, are uniformed and given a status (depending upon their importance) equivalent to the various active ranks. In the Army they are known by the general term, *Wehrmachtbeamten* but the Navy usually call them *Marinebeamten*.

Although, however, their uniforms are similar to those of the Officers and Men of the Service to which they are attached, there is always something—it may be a badge or a coloured piping—to show that they

are not actually commissioned. In the Navy it is a difference in the colour of the buttons and braid. Active ratings wear gold; *Marinebeamten* (officials), silver.

Ranks and their Equivalents

The following table will give some idea of the ratings and ranks, their approximate equivalents in our own Navy and the ranks to which they correspond in the German Army.

GERMAN NAVY	BRITISH NAVY	GERMAN ARMY
Matrose	Ordinary Seaman	*Schütze*
Matrosengefreiter	Able Seaman	*Gefreiter*
Seekadett	Cadet	*Fahnenjunker-Gefreiter*
Matrosenobergefreiter	Leading Seaman	*Obergefreiter*
Matrosenhauptgefreiter	Leading Seaman (4½ years)	*Hauptgefreite*
Bootsmannsmaat	Petty Officer	*Unteroffizier*
Fähnrich zur See	Midshipman	*Fähnrich*
Oberbootsmannsmaat	Chief Petty Officer	*Unterfeldwebel*
Bootsmann } *Stabsbootsmann* }	Boatswains	{ *Feldwebel* { *Stabsfeldwebel*
Oberfähnrich	Senior Midshipman	*Oberfähnrich*
Oberbootsmann } *Stabsoberbootsmann* }	Chief Boatswains	{ *Oberfeldwebel* { *Stabsoberfeldwebel*
*Leutnant zur See**	Sub-Lieutenant	*Leutnant*
*Oberleutnant z. See**	Lieutenant	*Oberleutnant*
Kapitänleutnant	Lieut.-Commander	*Hauptmann*

* *zur See* is the appellation of the Executive Branch. Theoretically all ranks should be so designated, but, for the sake of brevity I have shown it only after two of them.

GERMAN NAVY	BRITISH NAVY	GERMAN ARMY
Korvettenkapitän	Commander	*Major*
Fregattenkapitän ⎫	Captain	⎧ *Oberstleutant*
Kapitän zur See ⎭		⎩ *Oberst*
Konteradmiral	Rear-Admiral	*Generalmajor*
Vizeadmiral	Vice-Admiral	*Generalleutnant*
Admiral ⎫		⎧ *General der Inf.,*
Generaladmiral ⎬	Admiral	⎨ *Kav.*
⎭		⎩ *Generaloberst*
Grossadmiral	Admiral of the Fleet	*General-feldmarschall*

Badges of Rank

Petty Officers and Men

In the Army, a man's rank badge shows simply that he is a Lance-Corporal, Corporal, Sergeant, etc. Naval ratings, however, always wear two badges, one above the other. The lower one shows his grade, the upper, the Service Department or *Laufbahn* to which he belongs, and they are never worn separately.

The only exception is made in the case of recruits who have not made up their mind what they want to specialize in or who, having decided, have not yet completed their preliminary training ; they wear no *Laufbahn* badge. As soon as they are posted, however, they show the emblem of their trade on the left upper arm in yellow cloth or embroidery on blue jumpers, in cornflower blue on white ones.

Leading Seamen and Petty Officers' stripes mounted immediately below the *Laufbahn* badge are worked

THE NAVY

in the same colours, except on jackets, when they are made up in gold braid.

Here are the deck ratings :

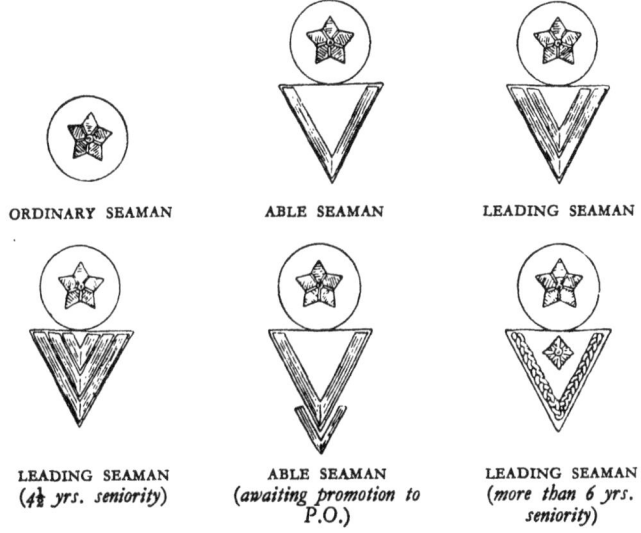

ORDINARY SEAMAN   ABLE SEAMAN   LEADING SEAMAN

LEADING SEAMAN   ABLE SEAMAN   LEADING SEAMAN
($4\frac{1}{2}$ yrs. seniority)   (awaiting promotion to P.O.)   (more than 6 yrs. seniority)

The last badge is made of flat plaited cord.

Petty Officers

An anchor is the distinguishing mark of Petty Officers and Senior Petty Officers ; for the latter, with a stripe added to it.

The anchor shown above is the form used for deck ratings, i.e. with rope attached.

Boatswains wear crossed anchors.

All other Departments have their trade emblem incorporated in the badge like this:

SIGNALMEN
(*Flag Letter C White, red border*)

TELEGRAPH-ISTS

CARPENTERS

ARMOURERS

TORPEDO ARTIFICERS

DEFENCE ORDNANCE ARTIFICERS (*Mines, etc.*)

AIRCRAFT SPOTTER

ADMINISTRA-TIVE PETTY OFFICERS

WRITERS

SICK BERTH PETTY OFFICERS

BANDSMEN

ENGINE-ROOM ARTIFICERS

RADIO TELEGRAPH-ISTS

GUNNERY PETTY OFFICERS

MOTOR-BOAT PETTY OFFICERS

ARMOURER

BOATSWAINS

Cadets

It has been explained that when a cadet enters the Navy he is a lower-deck rating and as such has no special privileges. While this is substantially true, he is, in fact, allowed to indicate that he is eventually destined for Officer's rank by wearing, instead of the trade badge of his shipmates, the emblem which is worn by the Officers of the Service arm for which he is entered.

There are six:

EXECUTIVE

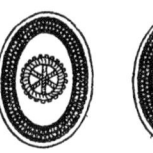
ENGINEERS   MEDICAL

ORDNANCE

ADMINISTRATIVE

Cadets undergoing training in Naval Construction wear the  *"Wehrmacht" Eagle.*

The badges are embroidered in gold on blue jumpers; blue on white uniforms.

Midshipmen

When a cadet is promoted to the rank of midshipman, he discards the fore-and-aft rig of the lower deck and, adopting the uniform of a Warrant Officer (although in actual fact as a junior Midshipman he rates only as a Petty Officer), he now shows his rank by silver shoulder cords and the badge of his *Laufbahn* in gold on his sleeve:

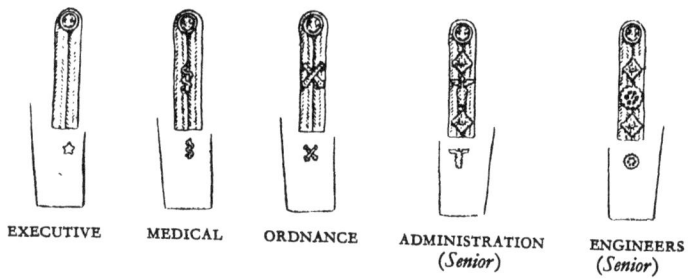

EXECUTIVE   MEDICAL   ORDNANCE   ADMINISTRATION (*Senior*)   ENGINEERS (*Senior*)

It will be seen that Executive Midshipmen wear their shoulder cords without ornamentation. The others show their *Laufbahn* badge. Senior Midshipmen mount two stars.

Warrant Officers

Other Warrant Officers wear shoulder-straps of dark-blue cloth bordered with gold braid, showing a miniature of their *Laufbahn* badge in gilt metal with the stars denoting their rank in silver. Since there are a greater number of steps in each Service branch than we have in our Navy, the German names are given rather than a possibly bad approximation.

THE NAVY

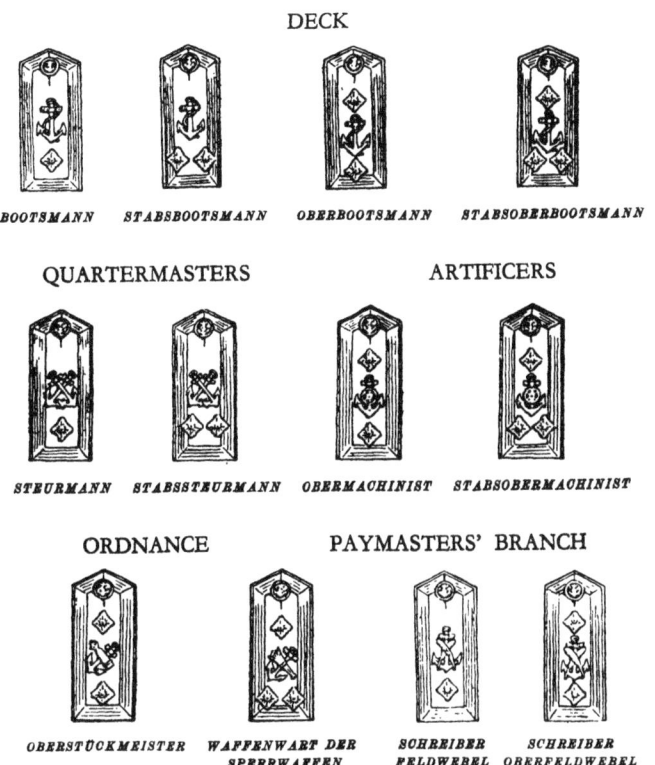

Ordnance Warrant Officers and Master Gunners have special *Laufbahn* badges. Administrative Officials wear none.

Officers

Commissioned Officers too wear shoulder-straps, but naturally, they are rather more elaborate, especially those worn by Admirals which show rank and *Laufbahn* badges in silver on a foundation of thick gold and silver plaited cord.

Those of the other Officers are simpler: gold badges on flat silver strands laid side by side (plaited for Captains).

Instead of shoulder-straps German Naval Officers, like our own, wear epaulettes with Full Dress. These also are made up in two different designs; for Admirals, with silver panels and gold badges; gold panels with silver badges for other Officers.

On Frock-Coats, Reefer Jackets and blue Mess Jackets there are further indications of rank in the shape of sleeve-rings of gold braid (silver for *Marinebeamten*). Reserve Officers add two oak-leaves.

Here are the epaulettes, shoulder-straps and sleeve rings of Executive Officers:

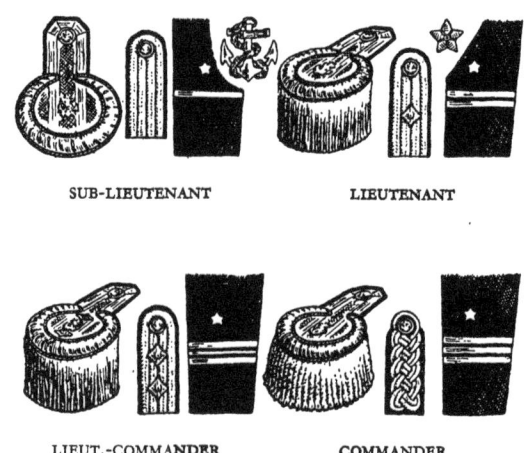

SUB-LIEUTENANT   LIEUTENANT

LIEUT.-COMMANDER   COMMANDER

THE NAVY

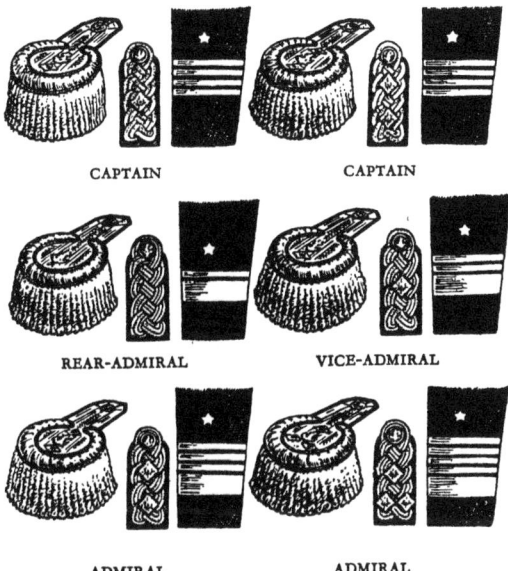

An Admiral of the Fleet wears crossed batons:

Except for the *Laufbahn* badges, the shoulder-straps and sleeve-rings worn by Officers in other branches are similar to those of the Executive Officers:

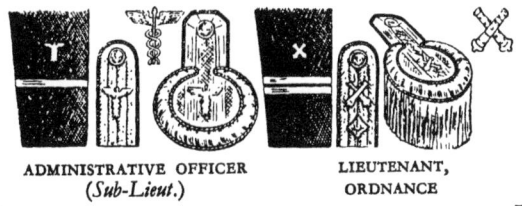

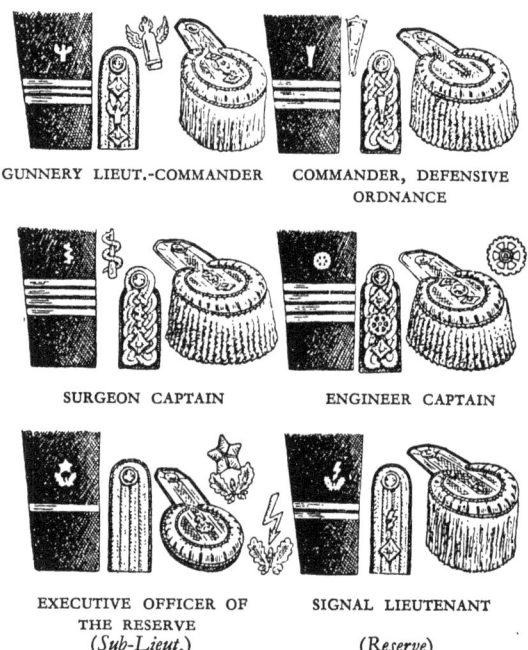

GUNNERY LIEUT.-COMMANDER   COMMANDER, DEFENSIVE ORDNANCE

SURGEON CAPTAIN   ENGINEER CAPTAIN

EXECUTIVE OFFICER OF THE RESERVE (*Sub-Lieut.*)   SIGNAL LIEUTENANT (*Reserve*)

Officers of the newly-instituted Signal Branch wear, as *Laufbahn* badge, a toothed wheel and lightning flash :

Musicians

Bandmasters and Music Directors wear the uniform of the Officers whose honorary rank they hold, but they never wear Full Dress epaulettes. Their ordinary

THE NAVY

shoulder-straps are of alternate strands of silver and dark-blue. Those of higher ranks are made up in plaited triple cord (two silver, one blue silk).

It is perhaps worth illustrating their sleeve-rings since they are quite different from those of regularly commissioned Officers.

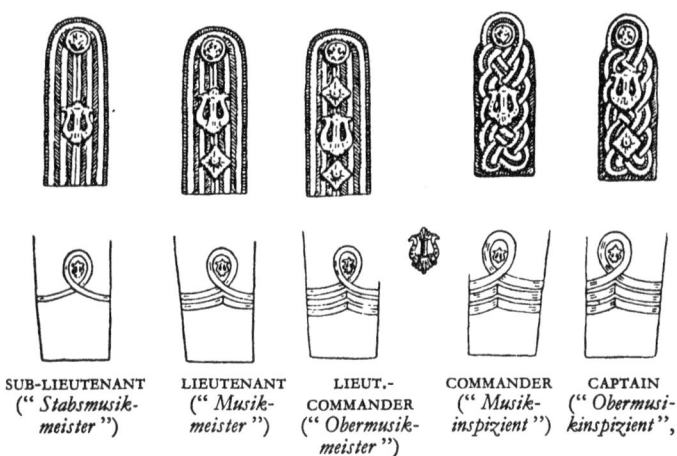

SUB-LIEUTENANT ("*Stabsmusikmeister*")   LIEUTENANT ("*Musikmeister*")   LIEUT.-COMMANDER ("*Obermusikmeister*")   COMMANDER ("*Musikinspizient*")   CAPTAIN ("*Obermusikinspizient*",

Uniforms

As is only right and proper, we, in this country, have set the fashion in naval uniforms for the rest of the world, and Germany, like everyone else, has followed our lead.

But, as is also understandable, she has interpreted the general idea according to her own taste, and so the German naval uniform, although one cannot exactly say why, is, if one may use the expression, typically German.

Perhaps, on the other hand, it is only because our own uniforms to-day are rather different from what they were thirty years before Nelson, and the German uniform, especially that of the lower-deck, has changed very little since then.

The various rigs as laid down in Naval Regulations are as follows :

Full Dress (for Officers only)
Parade Dress
Service Dress
Undress Uniform
Walking-Out Dress

Formal Uniform (for Officers only)
Formal Undress Uniform
Mess Dress
Tropical Uniform
Sports Rig

Let us start, as in the Army section with

CAPS

Petty Officers and Men

Lower-deck ratings, following the universal custom, wear a brimless cap with an interchangeable cap-band showing the name of the ship or shore detachment to which they belong.

Linienschiff Schleswig=Holstein
Panzerschiff Admiral Graf Spee
Kreuzer Köln
Torpedoboot Tiger
3. Schiffsstammabteilung der Nordsee 3.
2. Marineartillerieabteilung 2.

THE NAVY 85

For home waters it is navy-blue from the 20th September till the 20th of April; in summer and in the tropics, white.

The National Emblem and Cockade, worn above the cap-band, are of gilt metal.

Midshipmen and Warrant Officers

Midshipmen wear the same cap as Warrant Officers. Ordinarily blue, it has a white linen cover in summer.

The peak is black leather, the cap-band, mohair of the same colour, and the oak-leaves, gold for active Warrant Officers; silver for *Marinebeamte*.

Officers

On the Uniform Cap as worn by Officers, the peak is covered with navy-blue cloth ornamented with gold embroidery:

ADMIRALS AND COMMODORES
(*Captain wears a single row of the same embroidery*)

SUB-LIEUTENANTS, LIEUTENANTS,
AND LIEUT.-COMMANDERS

Badges are, as for Warrant Officers, in gold.

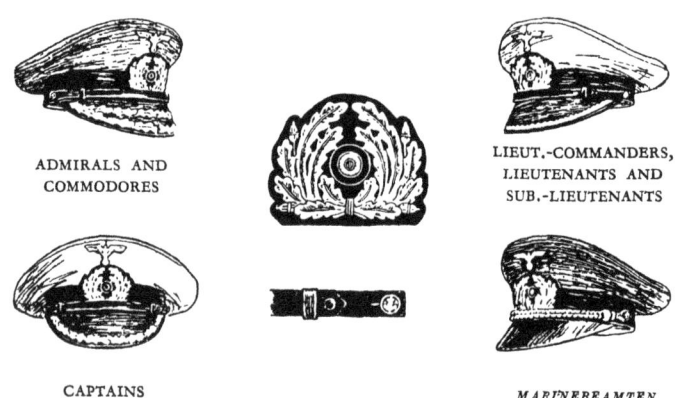

ADMIRALS AND COMMODORES

LIEUT.-COMMANDERS, LIEUTENANTS AND SUB.-LIEUTENANTS

CAPTAINS

MARINEBEAMTEN

Cap covers : navy-blue in winter, white in summer. Instead of chin-straps, *Marinebeamten* wear silver cords.

The Cocked Hat

A black felt Cocked Hat is used by Officers with Full Dress. It is ornamented with gold braid for

Admirals and Commodores, silver braid for *Marinebeamte* and black mohair for all other Officers. The Cockade is of black, white and red ribbon and the National Emblem is shown on a button at the side.

Uniforms

Petty Officers and Men

The Uniform most frequently worn by Petty Officers and Men of the German Navy is the same as our own—navy-blue Melton-cloth jumper with trousers of the same material. They have a white uniform as well, but its use is more circumscribed; it is worn mostly during the summer months, on Sundays and holidays and while home on leave.

A blue collar with three blue stripes and a " silk " accompanies both jumpers, the white one having, in addition, blue cuffs.

For fatigue duty aboard they are also issued with

Working Rig.

Of strong white ticking, this consists of a jumper (worn, however, as distinct from the blue and white ones, tight to the body) and trousers of the same material into which the jumper is tucked.

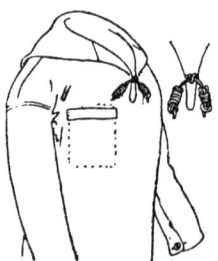

Petty Officers at work can generally be recognized by the fact that, instead of the full working rig, they usually wear only the trousers with the regulation blue jumper.

The Uniform Jacket

This is a purely German invention ; it has no equivalent in our own Navy.

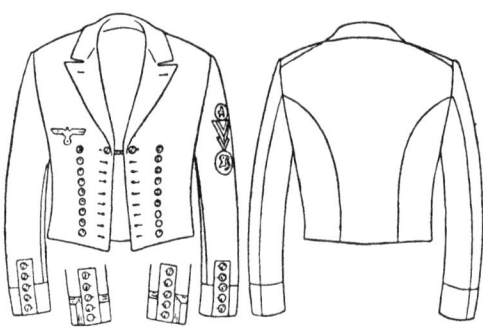

The Uniform Jacket is worn as Service Dress and

1. Signal Petty Officer. *Service Dress. Fleet Command.*
2. Quartermaster. *Service Dress as Watch-keeping Warrant Officer.* 
3. Lieutenant Commander, Marine Artillery. *Service Dress.* 
4. Commander. *Field Grey Service Dress.* 
5. Admiral. *Full-Dress with Aiguillettes.*

THE NAVY

Summer Walking-Out Uniform over either the blue or white jumper (collar outside).

Navy-blue with gilt anchor-embossed buttons and National Emblem worked in yellow silk, it shows, in the case of Petty Officers, gold braid on the cuffs in addition to their anchor rank badge.

Finally there is

The Pea Jacket

There is no Great Coat prescribed for Petty Officers and Men of the German Navy. They wear instead a Pea Jacket of thick navy-blue cloth. It is designed to go over the Uniform Jacket or the regulation jumpers (collar inside).

Buttons and National Emblem are the same as for the Uniform Jacket.

The collar-patches shown above are of cornflower blue with one strip of silver-braid for *Maate*, two for *Obermaate*.

Watches

On the larger ships, Petty Officers and Men indicate their Division and Watch by strips of red ribbon sewn high up on the upper arm.

STARBOARD
1st Division: one strip
3rd Division: two strips
5th Division: three strips
on the right arm.

PORT
2nd Division: one strip
4th Division: two strips
6th Division: three strips
on the left arm.

C.-in-C.'s Personnel

This badge denotes the immediate personnel of the Commander-in-Chief. It consists of a white

admiral's flag displaying an Iron Cross and is worn on the arm above all other badges.

Warrant Officers

All Warrant Officers, Midshipmen (including Midshipmen who have not yet reached Warrant rating) and *Marinebeamten* without Officers' rank wear navy-blue jackets and trousers of much the same cut as the working uniform of an officer.

THE NAVY

Since, except for a single-breasted white jacket for summer and the tropics, it is the only uniform they have, Warrant Officers wear it on all occasions :

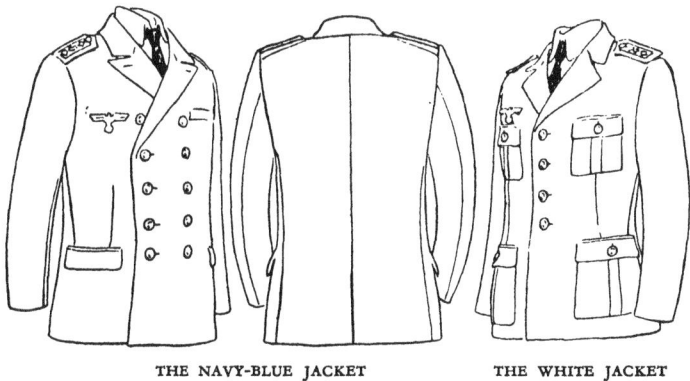

THE NAVY-BLUE JACKET   THE WHITE JACKET

Midshipmen, on the other hand, are privileged in that they have also a sort of Eton jacket, and, in the case of Senior Midshipmen, the Frock-Coat of a Commissioned Officer.

Marinebeamten can be distinguished from active ratings by the colour of their buttons and National Emblem, since they wear theirs in silver ; Warrant Officers are gilt.

A recent order lays down that in future the top button is to be left undone.

Officers

The Frock-Coat

" With epaulettes for Full Dress ; with shoulder-straps for Formal Uniform, Formal Undress Uniform,

Service Dress and Walking-Out Dress." This is the official description of the occasions prescribed for the Officers' Frock-Coat.

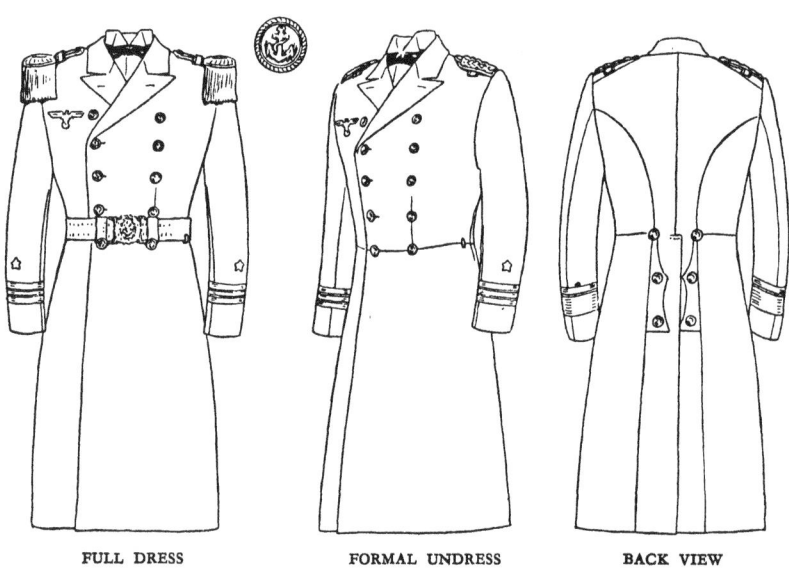

FULL DRESS　　　　FORMAL UNDRESS　　　　BACK VIEW

The coat is navy-blue with gold buttons embossed with an anchor, silver braided epaulettes or ordinary Officers' shoulder-straps, embroidered National Emblem and sleeve-rings with the badge of the Officer's Service Arm above them.

All accessories are gilt for active ranks, silver for *Marinebeamten*.

The trousers worn with the Frock-Coat have gold-braided side-seams.

Midshipmen wear the Frock-Coat only as Service Uniform and Walking-Out Dress, without epaulette attachments or sleeve-rings. They show their rank by shoulder-cords, their *Laufbahn* on the sleeve.

The everyday uniform of the German Naval Officer, however, is

The Blue Reefer Jacket

He wears it

On Parade ashore,
As Undress Uniform and for
Walking-Out on weekdays in Naval Bases, but *not* in Berlin.

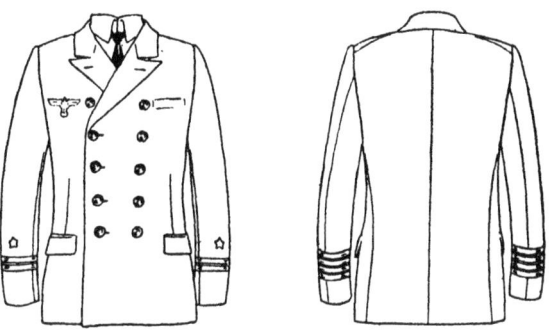

As worn by Officers, the Reefer Jacket differs from that of Warrant Officers in that it has no shoulder-straps. A turned down white collar and black tie go with it.

Anchor-embossed buttons, braid, rank badges and National Emblem are gilt for Active Officers and silver for Administrative Officials.

Trousers are the same as for full dress but without braid.

The White Jacket

In the tropics and during the summer months at home when lower-deck ratings are in white uniform or working-rig, Officers wear a white Uniform Jacket with patch pockets, shoulder-straps and gilt buttons.

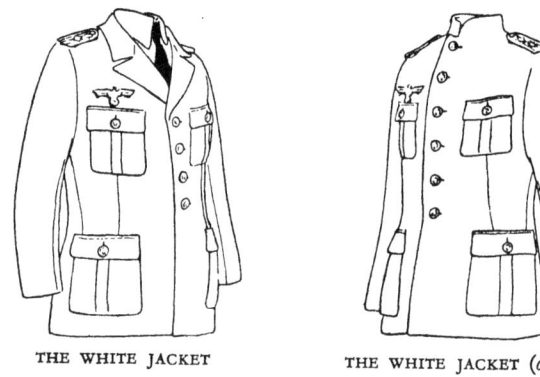

THE WHITE JACKET   THE WHITE JACKET (*old style*)

Ordinarily white trousers of the same material are worn with it, but sometimes during the winter time the White Jacket is used indoors, especially for office work, when it merely replaces the Blue Reefer.

Mess Kit

There are also two Mess Jackets, a blue and a white.

The waistcoat worn with it is usually of the same material and colour but on formal occasions the white one is prescribed.

Buttons, badges, etc., are gilt.

The drawings above illustrate the blue jacket; the white one has no sleeve-rings, rank badges being shown instead on shoulder-straps.

Great-Coats and Cloaks

All ranks from Warrant Officers (including junior Midshipmen) wear the same Great-Coat.

It is worn buttoned up except off-duty (or to display orders, etc.) when the three top buttons may be left unfastened.

Admirals have lapels of cornflower blue.

This cloak is not officially part of any of the uniforms mentioned, but it may be worn when no special dress has been prescribed.

AIGUILLETTES

Admirals, Commodores and *Marinebeamten* with Admiral's rank wear aiguillettes of gilt cord with Full Dress and Formal Uniform.

For Adjutants and Flag-Lieutenants there is a similar decoration but of simpler design. They wear it with all uniforms except Walking-Out Dress, but, when a number of Commanding Officers are present on any occasion, only the Adjutants of Flag-Officers and the Commander-in-Chief wear Aiguillettes.

FOR ADMIRALS, COMMODORES AND *MARINEBEAMTEN*

FOR ADJUTANTS AND FLAG-LIEUTENANTS

BADGE FOR WATCH-KEEPING OFFICERS

Watch-keeping Officers wear the badge shown above, on the Frock-Coat in the buttonhole of the left lapel ; on the Great Coat, in the second buttonhole from the top ; just above the top button on the left side of the Blue Reefer and in the buttonhole of the left breast pocket on the White Tunic.

CHAPLAINS

As in the Army, Chaplains are *Wehrmachbeamten* with the status of an Officer but without a definite rank.

They wear the ordinary *Marinebeamter's* cap but with a cross inserted between the Cockade and the National Emblem.

There are four uniforms ; a blue Frock-Coat with black cloth buttons, a Uniform Jacket with violet collar patches showing a Latin cross, a White Jacket and a White Mess Jacket, also with collar-patches.

Great-Coat with silver anchor buttons but no shoulder-straps.

Gloves, trousers and shoes as for Officers.

They carry no arms.

GLOVES AND SHOES

When gloves are worn, and in the German Navy that means a good deal more frequently than we do, they are usually grey (leather for Officers). But white ones are worn with Full Dress. When walking out, both Officers and Men have the choice of either grey or white.

Petty Officers and Men are issued with black boots, sea boots and canvas shoes. The sea boots, apart from their obvious utilitarian value, are also worn with Parade Dress; in summer with the trousers drawn up and turned down over them, in winter tucked into them. The canvas shoes are purely for light work on board or in barracks.

Officers have a wider and, to us, perhaps rather an incomprehensible choice of footwear. Black boots or shoes are usually worn but informally they may also wear brown ones, or patent leather boots are worn off-duty with white trousers and Formal Uniforms; white shoes are allowed only for work when white uniforms are being worn. Ashore, especially on manœuvres, they use black leather gaiters or Wellingtons.

Specialist Badges

Lower-deck ratings wear specialist badges on the left sleeve below their rank and *Laufbahn* badges. Here is a selection:

SEAMAN-GUNNER
(*Anti-aircraft, small calibre*)
(*3·7 c.mm. pom-pom, etc.*)

LEADING-SEAMAN GUNNER
(*Anti-aircraft, small calibre*)

GUNLAYER ANTI-AIRCRAFT

GUNLAYER " E "
(*Single gun*)

THE NAVY

GUNLAYER " T "
(turret) (2nd chevron for 3 years' seniority)

GUNLAYER " E "
(6 years' seniority)

GUNLAYER
(Coast Defence)

GUNNERY DIRECTOR

SMALL CALIBRE A.A. DIRECTOR

COAST DEFENCE ARTILLERY DIRECTOR

3RD-CLASS TORPEDOMAN

2ND-CLASS TORPEDOMAN

1ST-CLASS TORPEDOMAN

RANGE-TAKER

ANTI-AIRCRAFT RANGE-TAKER

TORPEDO-COXSWAIN

ASSISTANT TORPEDO INSTRUCTOR P.O.

MINELAYING AND BOOM-DEFENCE

BANDSMAN

HYDROGRAPHER ARTIFICER

DIVER

TORPEDO DIVER

ANTI-AIRCRAFT LISTENER

SEARCHLIGHT SPECIALIST

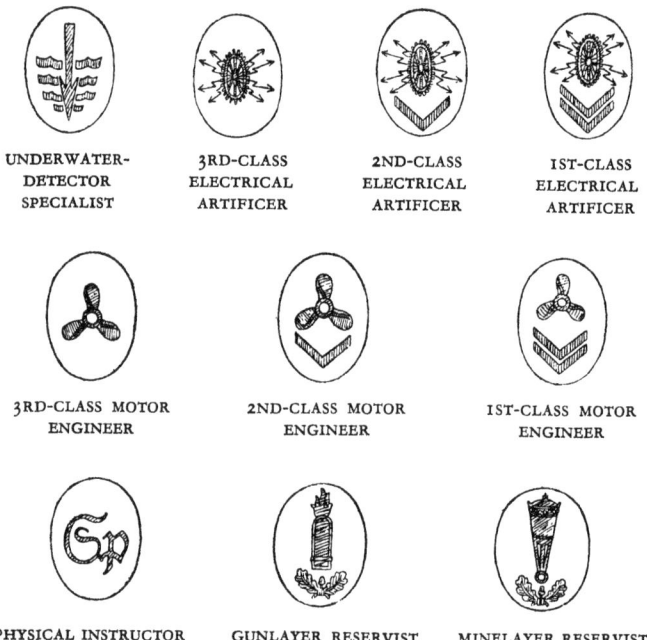

Marksman's Lanyard

The Navy, like the Army, awards special lanyards to its best marksmen. These vary in appearance according to the number of times they are won and with what type of weapon. A miniature acorn attached to the lanyard denotes a Machine Gunner or Rifleman ; a miniature winged-grenade an Anti-aircraft Machine-Gunner ; Gunlayers have a simple grenade and Torpedo Coxswains a small torpedo.

THE NAVY 101

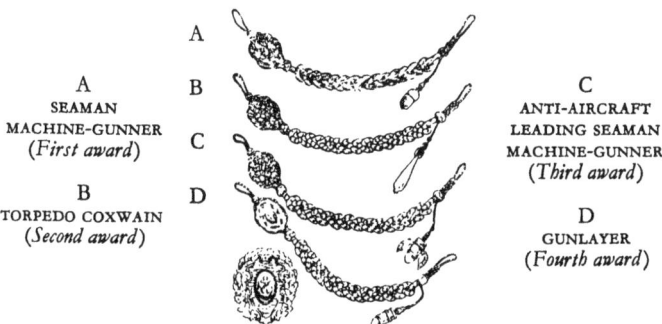

A
SEAMAN
MACHINE-GUNNER
(*First award*)

B
TORPEDO COXWAIN
(*Second award*)

C
ANTI-AIRCRAFT
LEADING SEAMAN
MACHINE-GUNNER
(*Third award*)

D
GUNLAYER
(*Fourth award*)

To indicate the number of times it has been won, the miniatures and the lanyard cord itself are variously coloured :

Acorns, grenades and torpedoes are :

> Gun metal for the first award.
> Silver-plated for the second award.
> Gilt for the third and fourth awards.

The Lanyard cords are :

Dark blue wool for the first award.
Dark blue worked with silver for the second and third awards.
Dark blue and silver with a gilt shield over the rosette (as illustrated) for the fourth award.

Various combinations of the lanyard and miniatures are possible. For example, a man who has won it once as a Seaman Machine-Gunner, once as an Anti-Aircraft Leading Seaman Machine-Gunner, and once as a Torpedo Coxswain, attaches an acorn, a grenade and a torpedo, all in gun metal, to a blue and silver lanyard (third award).

The Marksman's Lanyard is worn with Service Dress and Walking-Out Dress across the right breast.

Side-Arms and Portepees

Petty Officers and Men wear side-arms only when on Guard duty or when side-arms are specially prescribed. Belts and bayonets are the same as those worn by the Army except that the belt-buckle is gilt with a matt surface.

When Junior Midshipmen and Warrant Officers carry bayonets, they are slung either on a black leather belt or on one of the type mentioned above. Senior Midshipmen wear the Officers' brown leather belt.

As a general rule, however, Warrant Officers (and Midshipmen) wear a dirk. On Guard duty or when on parade ashore, they carry sword (Naval type).

Portepees

The *Portepee* is a tassel attached to side-arms, but, actually, it is more than that. To have reached the dignity of a *Portepee* is an indication that its wearer has passed beyond the rating of Petty Officer. In fact, as I mentioned earlier, the Germans have no generic term for either Warrant Officer or Petty Officer (or, for that matter, for N.C.O.s in the other Services) ; they are known respectively as *" Unteroffiziere mit Portepee "* and *" Unteroffiziere ohne* (without) *Portepee "*.

Midshipmen, as distinct from their corresponding ranks in the Army (Ensigns), wear *Portepees* only after having passed the examination qualifying them for Officers' rank.

From time to time, Commissioned Officers too have occasion to carry bayonets, but, like Warrant Officers, the side-arm they wear most frequently is the dirk.

With the ceremonial belt shown in the illustration to the Frock-Coat, the dirk is worn suspended by two straps.

With shoulder-straps and on parade ashore, sword is prescribed.

When one of the ancestors of an Officer in the direct line of descent has " carried his arms with honour in the face of the enemy " those arms, even though they may not measure up to the requirements of modern armoury, may, with special permission, be carried by his descendant.

The Field-Grey Uniform

Earlier in this section I mentioned with a proper satisfaction that most of the other countries in the world took the British Navy as a model when they came to design their own naval uniforms.

But in one respect at least the Germans took the bit between their teeth—when they decided to issue certain sections of their Navy with, in addition to blue and white rigs, a complete uniform in field-grey and one which the foreigner would find the greatest difficulty in distinguishing from the regular uniform of the Army.

However, there is a distinct justification for the innovation in that it is worn on land and only by certain special shore detachments. These include the Marine Artillery and lower-deck ratings undergoing training at shore establishments.

Since the uniform of the Army has been fully described in the first section of the book I will confine myself to mentioning briefly the details in which the naval field-grey uniform differs from it.

Steel Helmet

National Emblem ; matt gilt on a black shield.

Uniform Cap

Piping in dark blue-green ; National Emblem and oak-leaves for Officers, P.O.'s and Men in gold embroidery or gilt-metal ; silver for Administrative Officials.

Officers, Bandmasters, senior Midshipmen and Officials with Officers' rank wear silver cords instead of chin-straps.

Admirals do not wear the field-grey uniform.

1. Quartermaster. *(Warrant Officer.) Service Dress*
2. Chief Petty Officer *(Engine-room). Service Dress*
3. Chief Petty Officer, *Marine Artillery. Field Service Dress.*
4. Able Seaman. *Shore Parade Dress.*
5. Able Seaman Signaller. *Landing Rig*

THE NAVY 105

Field Tunic

Anchor-embossed buttons; braid wherever it appears, gold instead of silver; National Emblem as on the Blue Jacket.

Great-Coat

Anchor-embossed buttons.

Shoulder-Straps for P.O.'s and Men

Dark blue-green cloth; no piping; badges up to and including Chief Petty Officer in yellow wool; gold braid.

| ORDINARY SEAMAN, NORTH SEA FLEET | PETTY OFFICER ASPIRANT, BALTIC FLEET | PETTY OFFICER, 1ST DETACHMENT AIRCRAFT SPOTTERS | CHIEF PETTY OFFICER, P.O.'S INSTRUCTIONAL ESTABLISHMENT |

Warrant Officers wear slightly smaller badges in gilt metal; matt-gilt braid, silver stars.

| SERGEANT-MAJOR 2ND MARINE ARTILLERY | WARRANT OFFICER NORTH SEA FLEET | WARRANT OFFICER 4TH MARINE ARTILLERY | SENIOR WARRANT BALTIC FLEET |

SHOULDER-STRAPS FOR OFFICERS

Dark blue-green underlay for Active Officers, black for Reserve Officers; *Laufbahn* badges and rank stars only.

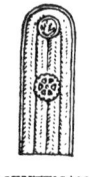
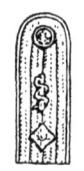

LIEUTENANT   SURGEON-LIEUTENANT   CAPTAIN

BELTS AND SIDE-ARMS

Belt as for blue uniform; Officers' brown leather belt without shoulder-strap.

Only Petty Officers and men of the Marine Artillery wear side-arm tassels (*Troddeln*).

Midshipmen, Warrant Officers and Officers wear, with bayonets, the Dirk *Portepee*. The dirk itself is never worn with the field-grey uniform.

TROUSERS AND GLOVES

Trousers without piping; Gloves as for blue uniform.

PART III

THE AIR FORCE

THE AIR FORCE

SINCE THE VERSAILLES TREATY forbade Germany to have an Air Force and it was Hitler, in March 1935, who recreated it, the German Air Force, or *Luftwaffe*, as it now stands, is by a very long way the newest of the three Services which comprise the *Wehrmacht*, and, to identify it closely with the party that brought it into being, the Nazis have designed a brand-new series of uniforms to go with it.

They have borrowed something from the Army (shoulder-straps and rank-badges) and something from the Navy (the White Uniform and the Mess Jacket), but there are also characteristic features which they owe to neither, i.e. the wing-badges on the collar-patches, their special version of the National Emblem and the general cut of the uniforms.

As in the other Services, the Air Force has its *Wehrmachtbeamten*—Administrative Officials attached to the Service—who in this country would probably rate as civilians, but who, in Germany, are uniformed and given ranks corresponding to those of Officers, etc. Others are equivalent to our Special Duties Branch.

The new *Luftwaffe*, however, has instituted an innovation in the Corps of Engineers and the Corps of Navigational Experts.

These are neither exactly active members of the Service nor *Wehrmachtbeamten* but come somewhere between the two.

So far as their ranks and uniforms are concerned the same policy has been adopted as with the Administrative Officials.

Organization of the " Luftwaffe "

The German Air Force is divided strategically into four Air Armies, i.e. Eastern, Western, Northern and South-Eastern; an Independent Air Force Command in East Prussia and two Air Defence Commands (Western Zone and Western Industrial Zone). Tactically there are six Divisions and a Training Division and the country is partitioned into eighteen Air Zones.

As in most Air Forces, there are nine machines to a Squadron (*Staffel*), three Squadrons to a Group (*Gruppe*), and three Groups to a Command (*Geschwader*).

Anti-Aircraft Artillery, which is an integral part of the *Luftwaffe*, is composed of Regiments, *Abteilungen* (see page 61), and Batteries.

The table which follows will give some idea of the actual distribution of the administration of the *Luftwaffe*.

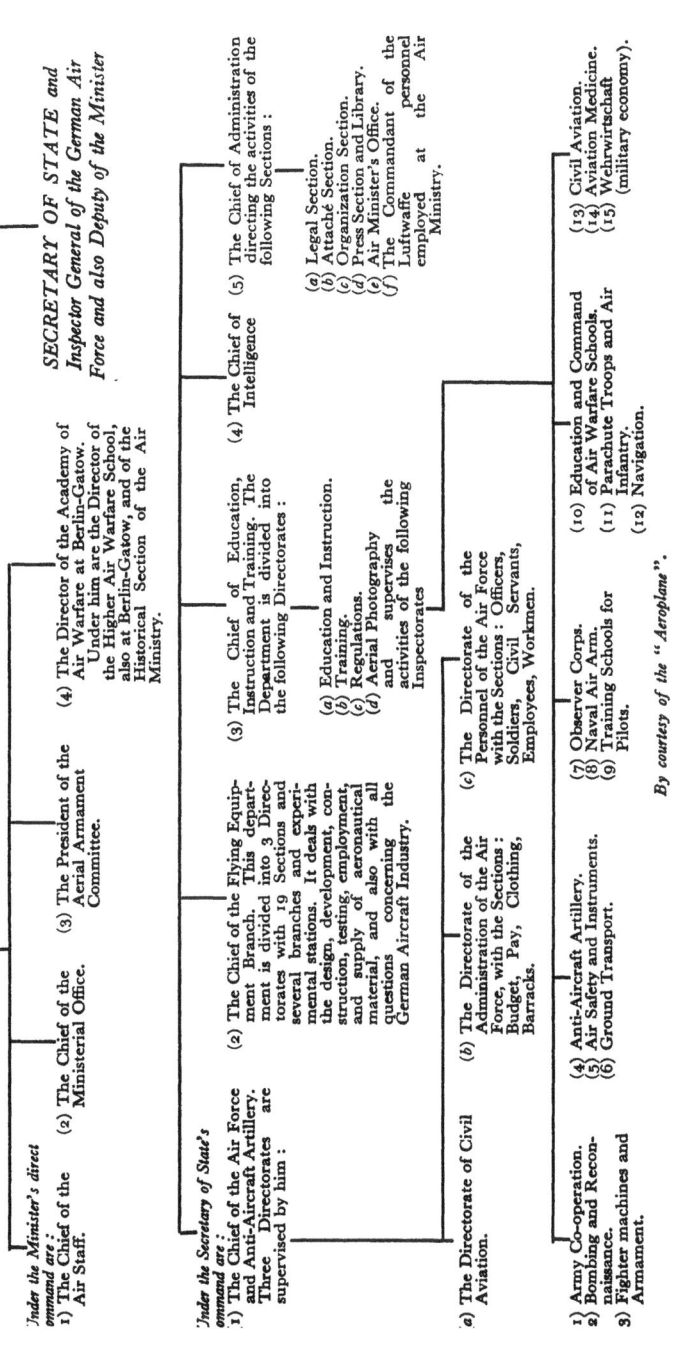

Ranks and their Equivalents

The ranks of the Air Force correspond, on the whole, to those of the Army with the following exceptions :

The lowest grade of Aircraftman is known as *Flieger, Kanonier* or *Funker.*

There is no *Oberschütze.*

Flight and Signals personnel call their Sergeants-Major *Feldwebel* ; Anti-Aircraft Sergeants-Major are *Wachmeister.*

Names like *Schirrmeister* and *Funkmeister* do not exist ; they are all known simply as Sergeant-Major, whatever their branch of the Service, with the exception of *Sanitätsfeldwebel* (Medical Warrant Officer) and *Feuerwerker* (Artificer Sergeant-Major).

The equivalents of *General der Infanterie* are *General der Flieger* and *General der Flakartillerie.*

The ranks of the *Luftwaffe* correspond to those of our Air Force as follows :

GERMAN	ENGLISH
Flieger	Aircraftman, 2nd Class
Gefreiter	Aircraftman, 1st Class
Fahnenjunker-Gefreiter	Flight Cadet Lance-Corporal
Obergefreiter	Leading Aircraftman
Hauptgefreiter	Corporal
Unteroffizier	Sergeant
*Fähnrich	Flight Ensign
Unterfeldwebel	Flight-Sergeant

* See " Ensigns " in the Army Section. The rank has the same significance in the Air Force.

1. General of the Air Force, Parade Dress. (Order: Grand Cross of the Crown of Italy)
2. Group Captain. Formal Full Dress (Evening)
3. Squadron Leader, Signals. Parade Dress.
4. Squadron Leader. General Staff
5. Surgeon Flight-Lieutenant. Undress Uniform with White Coat

THE AIR FORCE

GERMAN	ENGLISH
Feldwebel	
Oberfeldwebel	Warrant Officers and Senior
*Oberfähnrich	Flight-Ensign
Stabsfeldwebel	
Leutnant	Pilot Officer†
Oberleutnant	Flying Officer
Hauptmann	Flight Lieutenant
Major	Squadron Leader
Oberstleutnant	Wing Commander
Oberst	Group Captain
Generalmajor	Air Vice-Marshal
Generalleutnant	Air Marshal
General der Flieger	General of the Air Force†
and	and
General der Flakartillerie	General of Anti-Aircraft†
(No precise equivalent)	
Generaloberst	Air Chief Marshal
Generalfeldmarschall	Marshal of the Air Force

"Waffenfarben"

It might be advisable again to explain the term "Waffenfarbe".

Waffenfarben is the generic name for the colours given to the different branches of the Service to distinguish them from each other. It is used as piping, underlay on shoulder-straps, etc., and in the Air Force the colours are apportioned as follows:

White . . Air Vice-Marshal and upwards and for the General Goering Regiment

* See "Ensigns" in the Army Section. The rank has the same significance in the Air Force.

† It should be noted that there is no equivalent to our Acting P/O. or to our Air Commodore. On the other hand we have no General of the Air Force or General of Anti-Aircraft.

R.U.G.

Yellow . .	Flight personnel
Red . .	Artillery, Ordnance and Anti-Aircraft
Carmine .	General Staff
Rose . .	Engineer Corps
Orange. .	Half-pay Officers
Gold Brown .	Signals
Dark Blue .	Medical Corps
Light Green .	Aircraft Control
Dark Green .	*Wehrmachbeamten* (other than Aerodrome Control and Corps of Navigational Experts)
Black . .	Air Ministry

Additional colours are worn by the following :

Bright Red .	N.C.O.s and men of the General Goering Regiment, as an edging to the collar badges
Light Blue .	Officers, *Wehrmachtbeamten* and Engineers on the Reserve as piping on the collar and a second underlay to the shoulder-straps
Dark Red .	*Wehrmachtbeamten* of the Military Supreme Court, as second shoulder-strap underlay
Bright Red .	Other *Werhmachtbeamten*, as second shoulder-strap underlay
Yellow . .	Corps of Navigational Experts, as second shoulder-strap underlay

Badges of Rank

Men

As in the Army, N.C.O.'s wear their rank badges on the left upper-arm, but in the Air Force all ranks show, in addition, wings on the collar patches, like this :

THE AIR FORCE

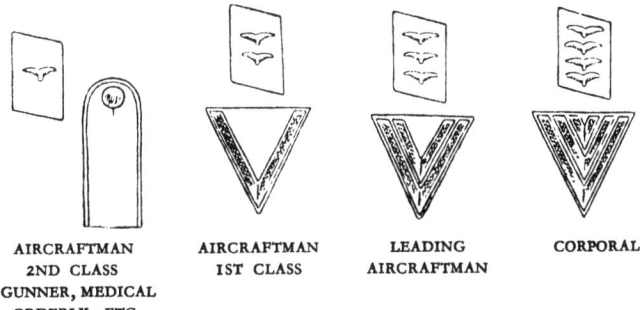

AIRCRAFTMAN 2ND CLASS
GUNNER, MEDICAL ORDERLY, ETC.

AIRCRAFTMAN 1ST CLASS

LEADING AIRCRAFTMAN

CORPORAL

The stripes are of silver braid on blue-green cloth, the wings white metal.

N.C.O.s and Warrant Officers

Senior N.C.O.s and Warrant Officers indicate their rank on shoulder-straps and by the number of wings on their collar-badges.

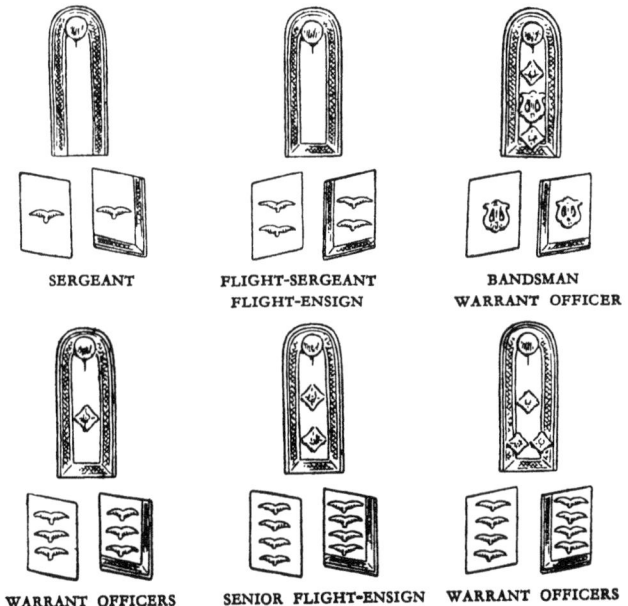

SERGEANT

FLIGHT-SERGEANT
FLIGHT-ENSIGN

BANDSMAN
WARRANT OFFICER

WARRANT OFFICERS

SENIOR FLIGHT-ENSIGN

WARRANT OFFICERS

Regimental badges on the shoulder-straps are, for N.C.O.s in *Waffenfarbe* ; for ranks from Senior Flight Ensign upwards, in white metal.

In addition (with the exception of Senior Flight Ensigns and certain other Warrant Officers who have the right to silver cords on the Uniform Cap) they show silver braid on the collar (two sides of the collar patches on the Great-Coat).

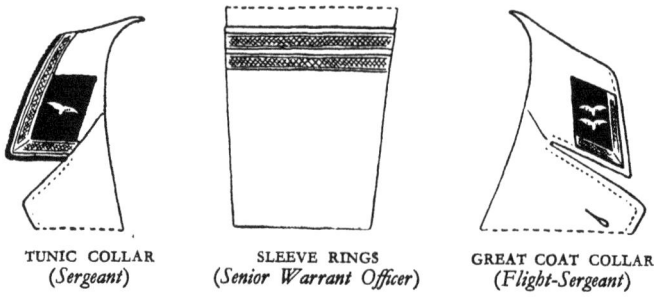

TUNIC COLLAR
(*Sergeant*)

SLEEVE RINGS
(*Senior Warrant Officer*)

GREAT COAT COLLAR
(*Flight-Sergeant*)

Senior Flight Ensigns and privileged Warrant Officers, instead of braid, wear silver cord.

Medical Warrant Officers show an Æsculapius rod between the stars ; Musicians, a lyre.

Officers

Officers, Officials and members of the two Corps indicate their rank on shoulder-straps.

For Officers from the rank of Air Vice-Marshal to Marshal of the Air Force they, and the badges on them, are gilt ; other ranks, silver. In addition, collar-badges of the former are edged with gilt cord ; the latter with silver cord.

THE AIR FORCE 117

Pilot Officers, Flying Officers and FlightLieutenants are known by two oak-leaves supporting the wings on their collar badges. Officers of higher rank surround them with a wreath of the same embroidery.

Instead of wings, *Wehrmachtbeamten* show triangular stars; Engineers and Navigational Experts, a propeller.

COLLAR BADGES OF OFFICERS

COLLAR-BADGES OF CORPS OF ENGINEERS, AND CORPS OF NAVIGATIONAL EXPERTS "*Wehrmachtbeamten.*"

Flight Lieutenant. *Group Captain or General of the Air Force.* *Marsha of the Air Force.* (*Group Captain rank.*) (*Flying Officer Rank.*)

Here is a complete list:

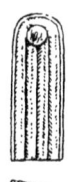 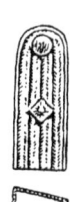  

PILOT OFFICER FLYING OFFICER FLIGHT LIEUTENANT SQUADRON-LEADER

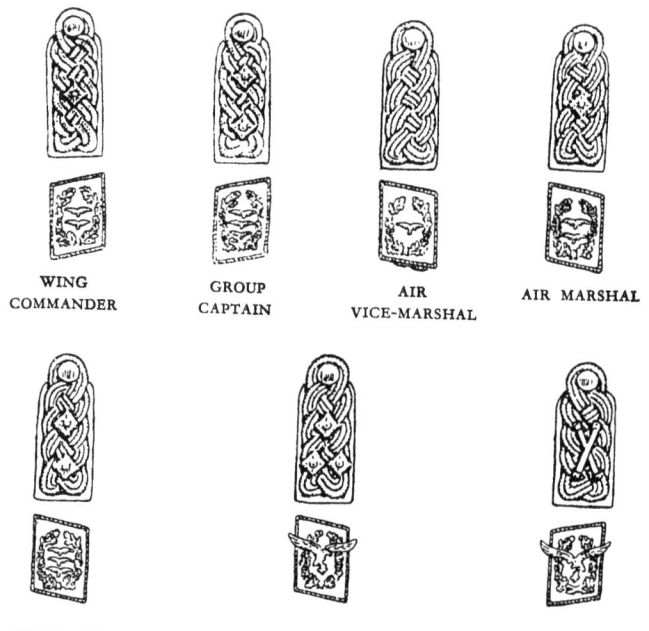

WING COMMANDER

GROUP CAPTAIN

AIR VICE-MARSHAL

AIR MARSHAL

GENERAL OF THE AIR FORCE (*extra rank— no British equivalent*), GENERAL OF ANTI-AIRCRAFT

AIR CHIEF MARSHAL

MARSHAL OF THE AIR FORCE

Shoulder-straps are made up in flat silver cord (plaited for Officers over the rank of Flying Officer). When unit numbers and letters are shown by N.C.O.s and men, Officers mount them also in addition to their stars, all of them being gilt.

Cord, numbers, letters and stars are built on a foundation of cloth in the *Waffenfarbe* (for Officers of the Reserve, a double underlay; the lower in *Waffenfarbe*, the upper light-blue; also a light-blue piping on their collar patches).

THE AIR FORCE 119

Corps of Engineers

Members of the Corps of Engineers who are on the Reserve use, in addition to the ordinary rose *Waffenfarbe* of their branch, a second underlay of light-blue on their shoulder-straps and a piping of the same colour on their collar badges.

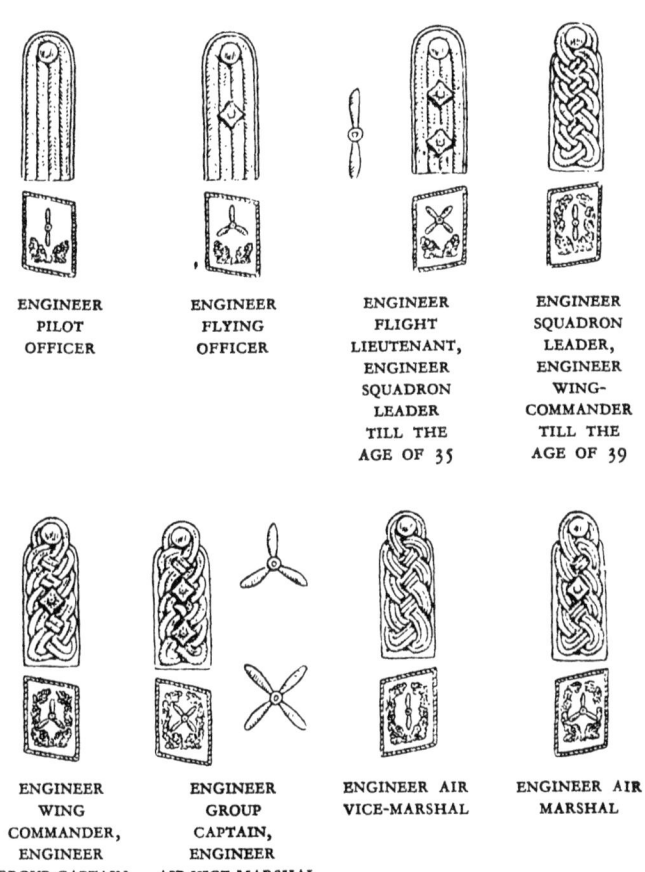

ENGINEER PILOT OFFICER

ENGINEER FLYING OFFICER

ENGINEER FLIGHT LIEUTENANT, ENGINEER SQUADRON LEADER TILL THE AGE OF 35

ENGINEER SQUADRON LEADER, ENGINEER WING-COMMANDER TILL THE AGE OF 39

ENGINEER WING COMMANDER, ENGINEER GROUP-CAPTAIN TILL THE AGE OF 39

ENGINEER GROUP CAPTAIN, ENGINEER AIR VICE-MARSHAL TILL THE AGE OF 45

ENGINEER AIR VICE-MARSHAL

ENGINEER AIR MARSHAL

Corps of Navigational Experts

The ranks and badges of the Corps of Navigational Experts are the same as those of the Corps of Engineers.

Their *Waffenfarbe* : dark green ; additional colour, yellow.

Medical Corps

Again following the custom of the Army, the Medical personnel of the Air Force show the rod of Æsculapius on their shoulder-straps.

WARRANT OFFICER
MEDICAL CORPS

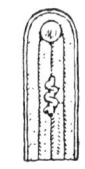
PILOT OFFICER
MEDICAL CORPS

AIR MARSHAL
MEDICAL CORPS

Officers up to the rank of Group Captain are distinguished by their *Waffenfarbe* of dark blue, with their badges in gilt. When serving in the reserve, however, they change to orange.

All senior surgeons, from Air Vice-Marshal upwards, use white as their *Waffenfarbe* and white-metal for their badges. Oddly enough, Warrant Officers, both active and reserve, have badges of the same colour.

Musicians

Officers and Men wear the uniform of the unit in which they are serving. The Officers have their collar badges and the underlay of their shoulder-straps

THE AIR FORCE

in the Musicians' *Waffenfarbe*. Their shoulder badges are in gilt.

Musikinspizients, equal to a Squadron Leader in rank, wear the uniform of Air Ministry Officers, their collar badges being decorated with a badge of lyre over wings.

The Officers' collar badges and shoulder-straps are as follows :

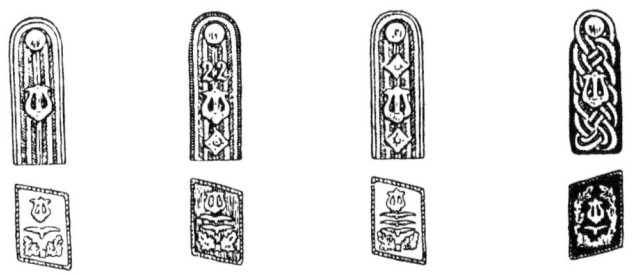

MUSIKMEISTER   OBERMUSIKMEISTER   STABSMUSIKMEISTER   MUSIKINSPIZIENT
(*Rank Equivalent* :   (*Flying Officer*)   (*Flight*   (*Squadron Leader*)
  Pilot Officer)   *Lieutenant*)   *Plaited of two silver*
The above are built up of half silver and half red, flat silk cord.   *and one red silk cord.*

SHOULDER-STRAPS

Men

Shoulder-straps for the ranks, which, as in the Army, do not show rank, are of blue-green cloth, the upper end being rounded and the whole piped in *Waffenfarbe*. When badges are worn, they are also in the distinguishing colour of the Service arm.

Here are the various *Waffenfarben*. Shoulder-straps with these colours are worn without badges by the following :

122   THE AIR FORCE

White .   .   General Goering Regiment
Yellow.   .   Air Force Group Commands, Air Force Commands, Air Zone Commands, Divisional Air Staffs, all schools not specially mentioned below and Drafting Units
Bright Red . Senior Officers of the Anti-Aircraft Artillery, Anti-Aircraft Station Staff personnel
Gold Brown . Signal personnel attached to Commands and Staff Headquarters, Signal Corps, Aerodrome Signal Stations, Aircraft Spotters
Light Green . Aerodrome Control
Black .   .   Ministry

Otherwise, shoulder-straps show the unit to which their wearer belongs like this :

Bright Red :   *Bright Red :*   *Yellow :*   *Gold-Brown :*
ANTI-AIRCRAFT   FORTRESS   GROUND STAFF,   SIGNALS SECTION
REGIMENTS   ANTI-AIRCRAFT   PHOTOGRAPHIC   OF THE AIR
                    ARTILLERY   DEPARTMENT OF   HIGH COMMAND
                                             THE AIR MINISTRY

 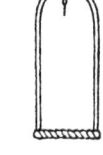  

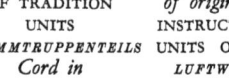

Yellow :   SHOULDER-STRAP   WAFFENFARBE   *Yellow :*
PERSONNEL OF   OF TRADITION   *of original unit*   RECONNAISSANCE
THE GUARD   UNITS   INSTRUCTIONAL   INSTRUCTIONAL
BATTALIONS OF   *STAMMTRUPPENTEILS*   UNITS OF THE   GROUPS
THE   *Cord in*   *LUFTWAFFE*
LUFTWAFFE   *WAFFENFARBE*

THE AIR FORCE

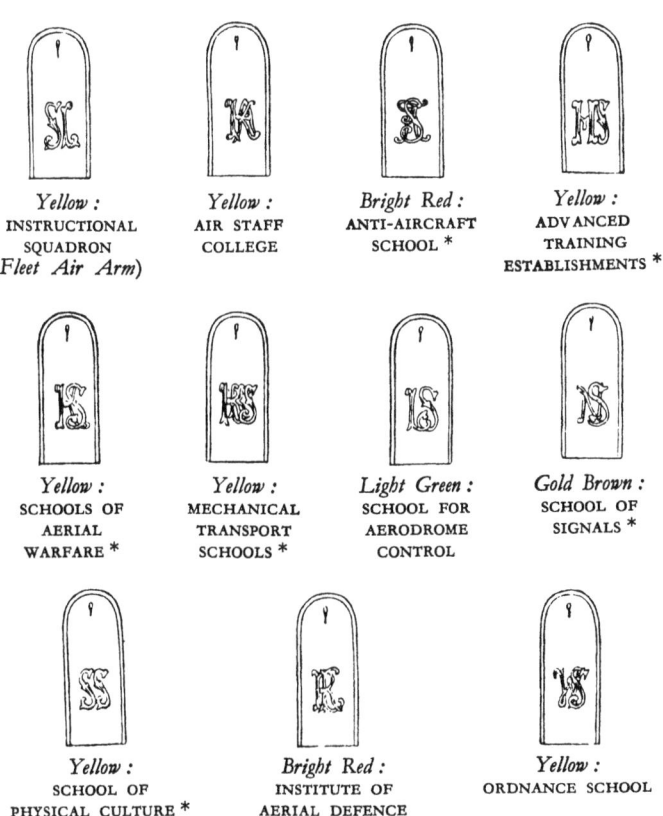

Yellow:
INSTRUCTIONAL
SQUADRON
(*Fleet Air Arm*)

Yellow:
AIR STAFF
COLLEGE

Bright Red:
ANTI-AIRCRAFT
SCHOOL *

Yellow:
ADVANCED
TRAINING
ESTABLISHMENTS *

Yellow:
SCHOOLS OF
AERIAL
WARFARE *

Yellow:
MECHANICAL
TRANSPORT
SCHOOLS *

Light Green:
SCHOOL FOR
AERODROME
CONTROL

Gold Brown:
SCHOOL OF
SIGNALS *

Yellow:
SCHOOL OF
PHYSICAL CULTURE *

Bright Red:
INSTITUTE OF
AERIAL DEFENCE

Yellow:
ORDNANCE SCHOOL

* Officers seconded to these Schools wear on their shoulder-straps *Waffenfarbe* of their original Unit with the badges of the School.

SPECIALIST BADGES

Non-Commissioned Officers and Men who have Specialist badges wear them on the left lower arm.

They are embroidered in matt-grey yarn on a foundation of the tunic-material and are as follows:

124   THE AIR FORCE

FLYING PERSONNEL (*except those who are entitled to a Pilot, Observer or Radio Operator's badge*)

TECHNICAL PERSONNEL

ADMINISTRATION N.C.O. | MECHANIZED TRANSPORT EQUIPMENT | EQUIPMENT BRANCH AIRCRAFT | SEARCHLIGHTS

SIGNAL EQUIPMENT BRANCH | QUALIFIED TELEPHONIST | QUALIFIED TELEPHONIST N.C.O. | QUALIFIED TELEGRAPHIST

QUALIFIED TELEGRAPHIST N.C.O. | QUALIFIED RADIO OPERATOR | QUALIFIED RADIO N.C.O. | QUALIFIED DIRECTIONAL RADIO OPERATOR

QUALIFIED LISTENING GEAR OPERATOR N.C.O. | SIGNALS PERSONNEL OF FLYING AND ANTI-AIRCRAFT BRANCHES | WARRANT OFFICER ARTIFICER | ORDNANCE N.C.O. (*Flying Branch*)

THE AIR FORCE

ORDNANCE N.C.O. (*Anti-Aircraft and General Goering Regiment*)   MEDICAL PERSONNEL   TRANSPORT DRIVER   ASPIRANT'S BADGE (*in this case awaiting promotion in Mechanized Transport Equipment Branch*)

ANTI-AIRCRAFT ARTILLERY BADGE   FLEET AIR ARM (*Ship's Personnel*)

THE MARKSMAN'S LANYARD

The method of awarding the Marksman's Lanyard is the same as in the Army and Navy. To keep it, it must be shot for regularly, successive awards being indicated by differences in the design as follows:

1st award. Lanyard in grey-blue silk decorated with silver
2nd ,,   as above; one dull-silver acorn
3rd ,,   ,,   ,,   two acorns
4th ,,   ,,   ,,   three acorns

5th ,,   Lanyard in silver decorated with grey-blue silk
6th ,,   as above; one bright silver acorn
7th ,,   ,,   ,,   two acorns
8th ,,   ,,   ,,   three acorns

9th   ,,   Lanyard in grey-blue silk decorated with old gold
10th   ,,   as above ; one old gold acorn
11th   ,,   ,,   ,,   two acorns
12th   ,,   ,,   ,,   three acorns

The shield, embossed with the Air Force eagle, matches, in each case, the colour of the acorns. Anti-Aircraft use miniature grenades.

STANDARD BEARERS

Standard Bearers wear a special badge on the right upper-arm. It consists of crossed standards, embroidered in the colours of their unit or in silver. Here are two examples :

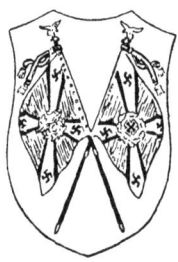 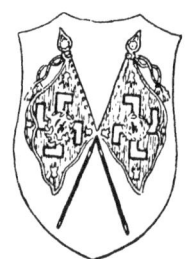

Musicians

Drum and Fife bands, Regimental bands and Buglers attach to their shoulders the type of shoulder-strap mentioned in the Army section under the name of " Swallows' Nests ". They are constructed in *Waffenfarbe* decorated with grey braid. Senior ranks have silver braid and fringes.

Commemoration Armlets

In the *Luftwaffe* of to-day the exploits of famous aces of the last war and of " heroes " of the Nazi Party are commemorated in squadrons bearing their names.

Members of these squadrons wear, attached to the upper-part of the right cuff, a dark blue band bearing the name of the squadron in silver embroidery.

Those who actually fought with the 1st *Richthofen* Fighting Command or the 2nd *Boelcke* Fighting Squadron have a special band which they may wear, provided the unit they now belong to has no commemorative badge of its own.

Members of the General Goering Regiment are decorated in the same way, but in the cases of Officers and N.C.O.s, with more elaboration. The former show a piping of bright silver in addition to the lettering ; the latter a matt edging of the same colour.

The only other unit with armlets piped in this way is the 1st Parachute Jäger-Regiment.

The name in this case, however, is worked on a foundation of light green.

Uniforms

While the Army and the Navy are by no means modest in their estimate of the number of uniforms required to ensure that they shall be suitably dressed

1 Second-Lieutenant, Anti-Aircraft Artillery. Formal Dress (Evening)
2 Pilot Officer. Undress Uniform with Forage Cap
3 Drum Major, General Goering Regiment. Parade Dress.
4 Sergeant-Pilot. Walking-out Dress.
5 Sergeant, Anti-Aircraft Artillery. Field Service Dress with Forage Cap

THE AIR FORCE 129

at all times, the Air Force, due possibly to the well-known proclivities of its first Commander-in-Chief, surpasses itself in this respect.

One might contrive to cover almost any occasion by the use of one of the following :

Flying Service Uniform for Flying Personnel
Field Dress
Service Dress
Guard Uniform
Undress Uniform for Officers and Leading N.C.O.s
Reporting Uniform
Parade Dress
Walking-Out Dress
Informal Full Dress (Day) for Officers
Formal Full Dress (Day) for Officers
Informal Full Dress (Evening) for Officers
Formal Full Dress (Evening) for Officers
Informal Full Dress for N.C.O.s and Men
Formal Full Dress for N.C.O.s and Men
Summer Uniform for Officers
Sports Kit

Wehrmachtbeamten and members of the Corps of Engineers and the Corps of Navigational Experts wear basically the same uniform as the rank the equivalent of which they hold.

Adopting the same order as in the first two sections let us start with the headgear.

In common with the other services, the *Luftwaffe* wears with Parade Dress, Field Dress and Guard Uniform.

THE STEEL HELMET

It is of the characteristic shape used in all branches of the *Wehrmacht* but, instead of field-grey, it is coloured, like the uniform, in the shade we know as Air Force Blue.

The National Emblem appearing on the right side is the special eagle of the *Luftwaffe* ; the shield on the left the same as on the Army and Navy Steel Helmet, i.e. barred in the national colours (black, white and red).

For Air Vice-Marshals and upwards and Engineers with those ranks, the eagle is gilt ; for others, silver-grey.

THE UNIFORM CAP

Also of Air Force blue, the Uniform cap is worn :

With Service Dress and Undress uniform by Officers and N.C.O.s.
With Parade Dress, by Officers when not actually on duty.
With Walking-Out Dress and with Dress uniforms by Officers.

  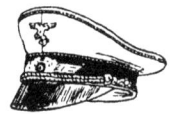

FOR N.C.O.S AND MEN   FOR OFFICERS

The National Emblem is shown on the front of the cap-cover, and the Cockade (black, white and red), surrounded by oak-leaves and flanked by wings, on the black mohair cap-band.

N.C.O.s and men wear piping in *Waffenfarbe* round the cap-cover and a black patent-leather chin-strap. Their National Emblem and Cockade are stamped out of aluminium.

Senior Flight Ensigns, Medical Warrant Officers, Warrant Officer Artificers and *Wehrmachtbeamten* with warrant rank wear, instead of chin-straps, silver cords; their Emblem, oak-leaves and wings are on issue caps, the same as for N.C.O.s and men; in silver embroidery on their own.

For Officers, all decorations (including piping and cords) are silver; Air Vice-Marshals and upwards in gold.

THE FORAGE CAP

For such occasions as are not covered by the Steel Helmet and the Uniform Cap all ranks wear the Forage Cap.

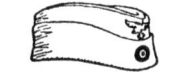 

FOR N.C.O.S AND MEN   FOR OFFICERS

The Cap differs for Officers, *Wehrmachtbeamten*, the two corps and those Warrant Officers who are entitled to silver cords on the Uniform Cap only, in that it has a piping of silver cord round the upper edge of the turn-up.

The National Emblem is embroidered in matt grey except in the case of officers of the rank of Air Vice-Marshal and upwards. For them both piping and emblem are gilt.

Tunics

When the new Air Force was first inaugurated, Officers, N.C.O.s and Men had both a Service Tunic and a Flying Service Tunic. Lately, however, a Uniform Tunic has been designed which embodies the features of both and will eventually replace them. Probably the issue has been completed, but in case there are some of the old ones still in service this is what they look like.

The Service Tunic

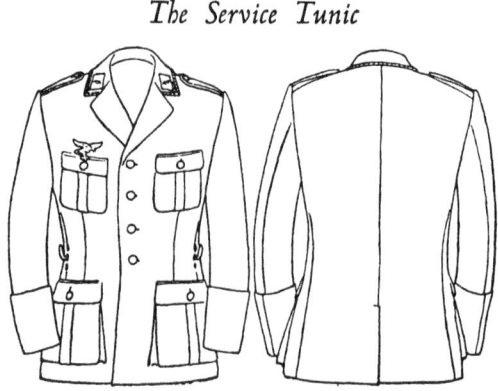

The Tunic, including collar and cuffs, is Air Force blue with aluminium buttons.

Officers, Senior Flight Ensigns and privileged Warrant Officers are distinguished from N.C.O.s and Men by the colour of their collar piping. They wear silver ; N.C.O.s and Men wear their *Waffenfarbe*. Shoulder-straps vary according to the rank, Service Arm and Unit.

The special Air Force version of the National

Emblem, worn on the right breast, is, for N.C.O.s and Men, machined in grey yarn, but it may be hand-embroidered on non-issue tunics ; for Officers, it is worked in silver thread.

The usual differences are made in the case of ranks from Air Vice-Marshal to Marshal of the Air Force. Their buttons, collar-piping and National Emblem are gilt instead of silver. With the tunic a blue shirt, turned-down collar and black tie are worn.

According to official regulations, the order prescribed for the wearing of the Service Tunic is as follows :

With Parade Dress . . For Officers and Warrant Officers
  ,, Service Dress . .⎫
  ,, Undress Uniform . .⎬ For Officers
  ,, Reporting Uniform .⎭

With Walking-Out Dress	White shirt and collar may be worn
,, Flying Service Uniform.	In place of the Flying Service Tunic
,, Formal and Informal Full Dress for N.C.O.s and Men	With white shirt, stiff collar and black tie
,, Formal and Informal Full Dress (Day) for Officers	

The Flying Service Tunic

The Flying Service Tunic is worn with collar open or closed by N.C.O.s and Men.

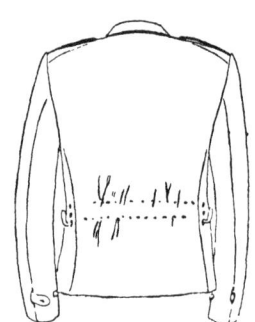

Worn by officers,

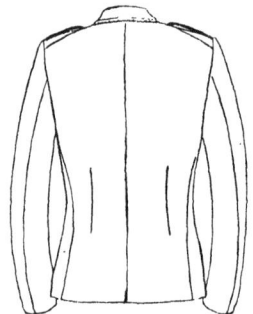

it is used

With Flying Service Uniform
With Field Dress
With Undress Uniform for Senior Warrant Officers, and
With Undress Uniform for Officers in place of the Service Tunic

Ordinary Warrant Officers, N.C.O.s and Men do not show the National Emblem on the Flying Service Tunic. Although this Tunic will shortly become obsolete as part of the regular uniform of the *Luftwaffe*, it will still be used by officers, *Wehrmachtbeamten* and the two Corps for office work and light duties.

The Uniform Tunic

The principal difference in the new Uniform Tunic is that it has an extra button and the collar is cut in such a way that it can be worn either open or closed.

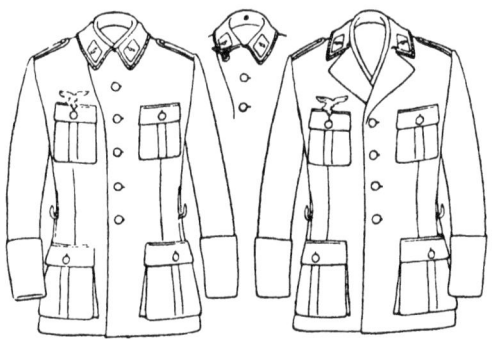

Otherwise, buttons, badges, collar patches, etc. etc., the same as for the Service Tunic.

Special Tunic for Air Marshals

Officers of the rank of Air Vice-Marshal and upward have a special tunic with white lapels and white piping on the sleeves and front overlap which they use with Walking-Out Dress, Undress and Informal Full-Dress Uniforms. Badges, etc., are the same as for the Uniform Tunic.

The Summer Tunic for Officers

From the 1st of April till the 30th of September, Officers of the *Luftwaffe*, *Wehrmachtbeamten* with officers' rank and members of the two Corps wear, with Walking-Out Dress, Undress Uniform and Full Dress (day), a white tunic with either a blue or white shirt (white for Full Dress).

Badges, shoulder-straps and buttons are those of the Uniform Tunic, except that the National Emblem is usually of white-metal (gold for Marshals), made to be pinned on.

Evening Full Dress for Officers

The Mess Jacket, used with both Informal Evening Full Dress (blue waistcoat and black tie) and Formal Evening Full Dress (aiguillettes, white waistcoat and

THE AIR FORCE

white tie) is similar in cut to that of the officers of the Navy.

Air Force blue in colour, it is worn with peaked collar and stiff shirt with mother-of-pearl studs. All badges, buttons, etc., are the same as those worn with the Uniform Tunic. A new regulation permits the Day Full Dress to be used in the evening and, in summer, the White Tunic.

AIGUILLETTES

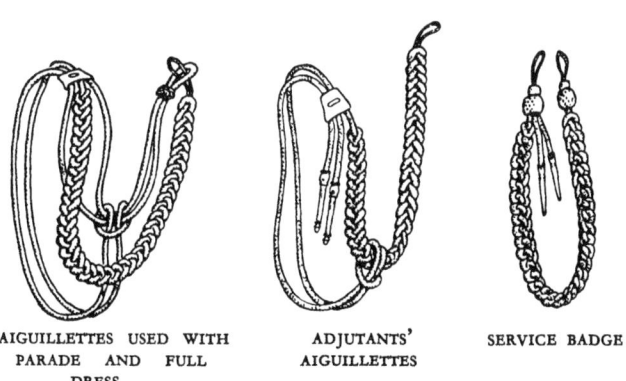

AIGUILLETTES USED WITH PARADE AND FULL DRESS

ADJUTANTS' AIGUILLETTES

SERVICE BADGE

With Parade Dress and with Day and Evening Full Dress, Officers, Engineers, Navigational Experts,

Wehrmachtbeamten with officers' rank and Music Directors wear *aiguillettes*.

Attached from the right shoulder to the top Tunic button, they are silver for ranks from Pilot Officer to Group Captain ; for Marshals, gold, in the style of an Admiral's *aiguillettes*.

The Adjutant's aiguillettes, also silver, are for use with Field Dress, Reporting Uniform, Service Dress and Parade Dress. With the last-named, however, they are attached only to the Great-Coat since naturally both types of aiguillettes cannot be worn at the same time on the tunic.

The Lanyard shown in the third illustration, known as a *Dienstabzeichen* (Service Badge), is worn while on duty by Officers and N.C.O.s engaged in the various contributory branches of the Air Force, e.g. Transport Officers and N.C.O.s, Telegraphists, Aircraft Directional Radio Operators, etc. The ends are attached under the right shoulder-strap.

Coats

The same form of Great-Coat is worn by all ranks ; it is Air Force blue with collar badges and shoulder-straps. It can be worn open or closed.

Only for Marshals is it somewhat different. Their lapels are in *Waffenfarbe* (white), the colour being continued in the form of piping down the front overlap to the bottom of the coat.

Waterproofs and Leather Coats for Officers are also

in Air Force blue, cut like the Great-Coat. Their shoulder-straps are detachable.

Cloaks

Air Force Officers seem to have a greater liking for cloaks than either the Army or the Navy. They have them of both cloth and rubberized material. So long as a definite dress has not been prescribed for the day, they may be worn with all uniforms. They are also worn over the Great-Coats.

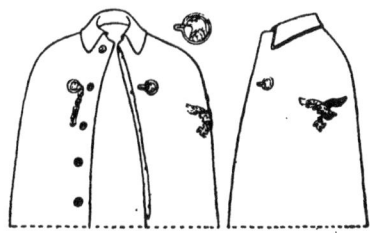

In the prevailing colour of all uniforms, they are fastened by a chain attached to eagle-embossed ornaments of oxydized white-metal.

The National Emblem, larger than those on tunics, is embroidered in silver.

For Marshals, the collar has a white piping and under-surface and all decorations are gilt.

Working Uniform

A two-piece uniform of strong black ticking is issued to N.C.O.s and Men for rough work. Rank badges are shown on the arm and where collar-braid is worn on the Uniform Tunic, on this uniform it is of Air Force blue.

The four grades of Warrant Officer indicate their rank by sleeve-rings as follows :

Flying Uniform

There are three Flying Uniforms ; for Land, the Fleet Air Arm and a lighter weight for Summer.

THE AIR FORCE

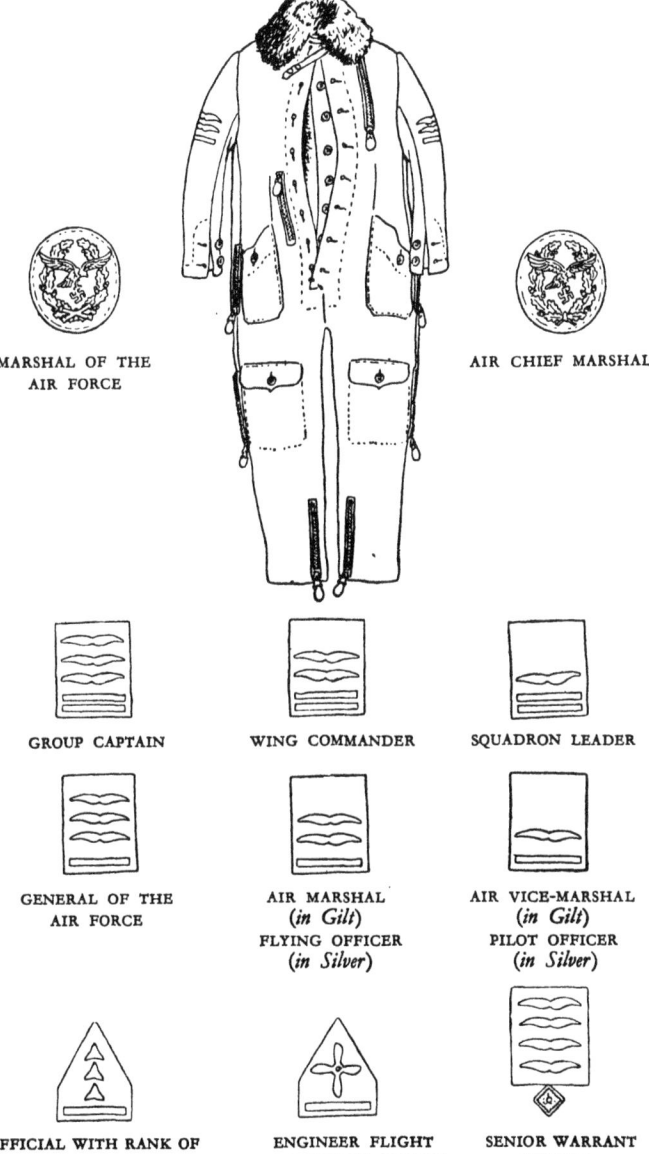

MARSHAL OF THE
AIR FORCE

AIR CHIEF MARSHAL

GROUP CAPTAIN

WING COMMANDER

SQUADRON LEADER

GENERAL OF THE
AIR FORCE

AIR MARSHAL
(*in Gilt*)
FLYING OFFICER
(*in Silver*)

AIR VICE-MARSHAL
(*in Gilt*)
PILOT OFFICER
(*in Silver*)

OFFICIAL WITH RANK OF
FLIGHT LIEUTENANT

ENGINEER FLIGHT
LIEUTENANT, FLIGHT
LIEUTENANT CORPS OF
NAVIGATIONAL EXPERTS

SENIOR WARRANT
OFFICER

THE AIR FORCE

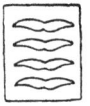
WARRANT OFFICERS

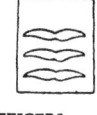
FLIGHT SERGEANT

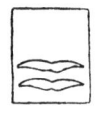

SERGEANT

Waterproof Coat for Motorized Units

The Waterproof Coat differs from that of the Army in that it has no shoulder-straps.

SHOULDER-STRAPS ON ARMY WATERPROOF COAT

OFFICERS' ARM-BADGES ON AIR FORCE COAT

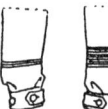
WARRANT OFFICERS

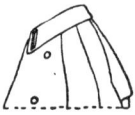
N.C.O.S

The rank of N.C.O.s is indicated by badges of grey braid on the collar; of Warrant Officers by sleeve-rings.

Officers wear badges as for the Flying Uniform.

Mountain Equipment

Certain units of Anti-Aircraft and Signallers wear a Mountain Cap like the Mountain Cap of the Army, except that it is Air Force blue and shows the *Luftwaffe* version of the National Emblem.

This Cap may be worn by all ranks of the Air Force for Winter Sports.

With the Mountain Cap is worn a Wind Jacket and climbing boots.

Special Equipment of Parachute Troops

Parachute Troops wear a flying suit which closely resembles the one already described and a Steel Helmet of special design.

"Faustriemen" and "Portepees"

In the Army section of this book there is a full description of the various colourings of the tassels attached to side-arms (called *Faustriemen* for N.C.O.s, *Portepees* for higher ranks) and an explanation of their significance.

Remembering that the Flying Branch is divided into Squadrons, Groups and Commands, the Anti-Aircraft into Batteries, *Abteilungen* and Regiments and the Signals into Companies and Brigades, the method of distinguishing these units on the *Faustriemen* of the *Luftwaffe* is the same as in the Army.

The apportioning of the colours is as follows:

Dark Green	Headquarters
White	1st Unit
Red	2nd ,,
Yellow	3rd ,,
Cornflower Blue	4th ,,
Gold Brown	5th ,,
Rose	6th ,,

The actual tassel of the *Faustriemen* is Air Force blue for Squadrons, Batteries and Companies. Otherwise the system followed is that previously described.

Flight Cadet Lance-Corporals, Sergeants and Flight-Sergeants wear a special N.C.O.'s *Faustriemen* with an Air Force blue strap and Top, green Crown decorated with silver and a Tassel of silver cord.

The *Portepee* distinguishes ranks from Senior Flight-Ensign upwards. It is in the form of the Army Dirk *Portepee*, entirely of silver.

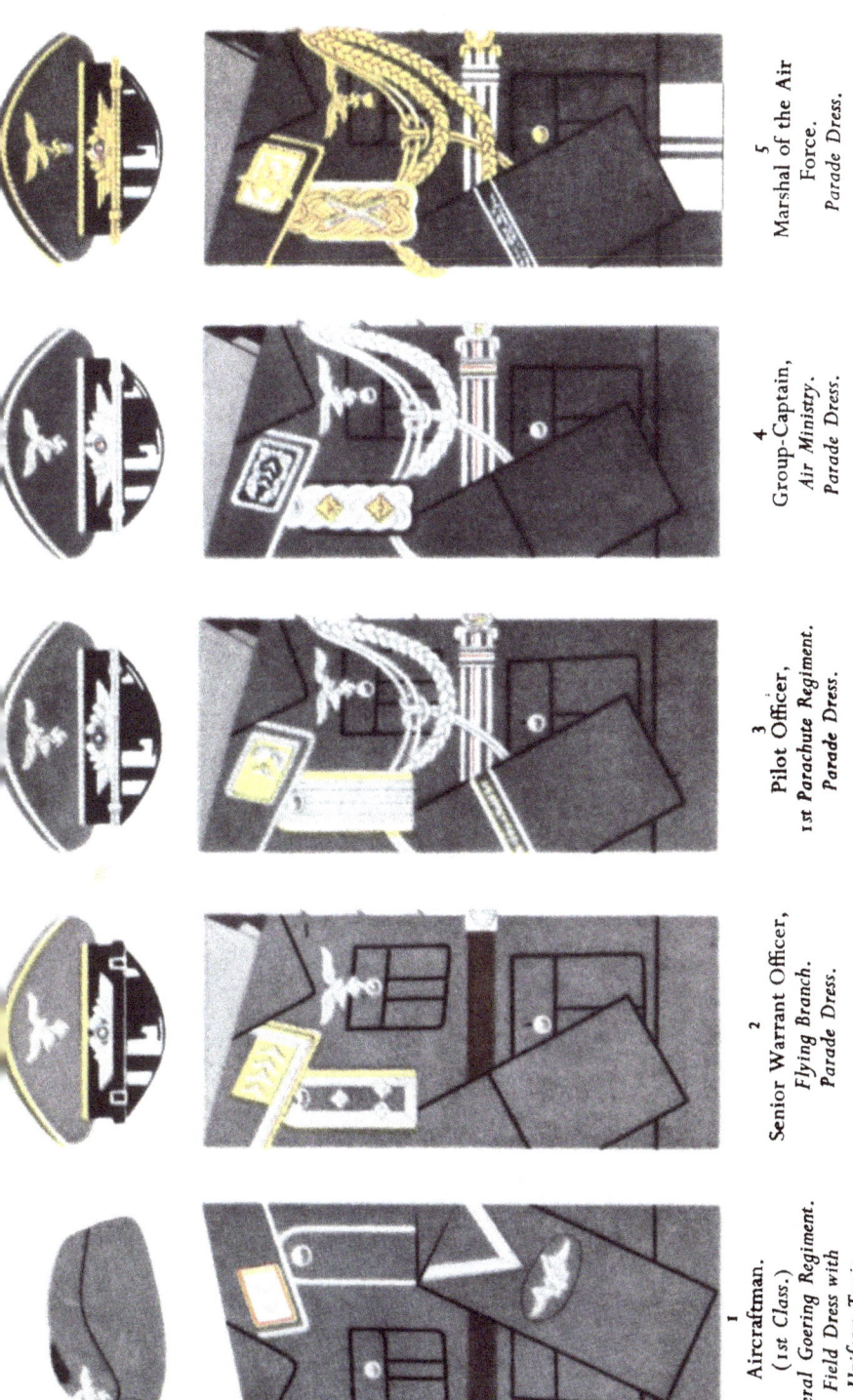

Side-Arms

Generally speaking, N.C.O.s and Men carry as side-arm with all uniforms the Bayonet, slung on a dark-brown belt and showing the *Faustriemen* of their unit.

But those who, belonging to the actual Flying Branch, are in possession of a Pilot, Observer or Radio-Operator's badge, wear, instead, a Dirk (Air Force model). No side-arm tassel is attached to it however, except by Flight Ensigns, who show their *Portepees*.

For Warrant Officers, Dirk, Bayonet or Sword are in order.

The Sword, worn with Field Dress, is attached to a special frog, through the left pocket of the tunic, to a belt worn underneath it. The Bayonet is used with Field Uniform and the Dirk when in Walking-Out Dress.

With Undress Uniform any one of the three may be worn.

Senior Flight Ensigns and those privileged Warrant Officers mentioned earlier have, instead of the plain dark-brown belt, a special type worn by Officers, i.e. light-brown in colour with a strap over the shoulder (rather like what we know as a Sam Browne). They attach to it the Officers' Dirk.

This is the principal side-arm worn by Officers, although they also, on occasion, carry Bayonet and Sword. All are attached either to the Sam Browne belt mentioned above or, in the case of the Sword (with Service Dress, Reporting Uniform and Parade

Dress) and the Dirk (with Full Dress), to a belt constructed of a sort of silver braid.

Marshals have a special Short Sword which they wear with Undress Uniform, Walking-Out Dress and Informal Full Dress (Day). To it is attached a *Portepee* which, incidentally, is never shown on the regulation full-length Swords.

Trousers

Slacks in cloth of Air Force blue are worn by all ranks; trousers of the type known as *Flieger-hosen* by N.C.O.s and Men and breeches by Officers, *Wehrmachtbeamten* with Officer's rank, the two Corps and those Warrant Officers who are responsible for their own uniforms.

Marshals and General Staff Officers brighten theirs with a broad stripe of their *Waffenfarbe* down the side-seams of both breeches and slacks.

With Evening Full Dress, Officers up to the rank of Air Vice-Marshal show similar stripes in silver braid, Marshals in gold.

Footwear

Boots and Wellingtons are the regulation footwear of the *Luftwaffe*, although shoes are allowed with Walking-Out Dress, Undress and Formal Uniforms.

Three-quarter length Marching Boots for N.C.O.s

THE AIR FORCE 147

and Men and Field Boots for Officers are the regulation footwear in the field, although ordinary boots and shoes are permitted with Walking-Out Dress, Undress Uniform and Formal Uniforms.

In summer, Officers may use white shoes with their White Uniforms, but N.C.O.s and Men are restricted to black.

It may be that this book has given the impression that the Germans take their uniforms more seriously than we do. If additional evidence were required to support this view it would only be necessary to glance through the official *Regulations relating to the Order of Uniforms for Special Occasions*. This consists of a series of the most meticulous directions as to what should be worn when attending various functions.

It is inclined to be repetitive and is not really worth reproducing, but there are one or two of the section-headings of which I am particularly fond. One paragraph, for example, describes how one must dress " *When Attending the Laying of Foundation Stones* ". Further on there are sections dealing with the uniforms to be worn at *Race Meetings, Concerts, Unveiling of Memorials, Dedications of Buildings, etc.*

In fact, in Germany, the fighting man is in the happy position of finding it quite unnecessary to use his own judgment, even in the apparently simple matter of what to wear and when to wear it.

GLOSSARY

GLOSSARY

This glossary does not pretend to be exhaustive. It has been included merely for the purpose of giving the equivalents of some of the more significant words and phrases used in the book. But it may be that the word or expression you want is there even though you do not find it straight away.

Germans have a carefree habit of taking a string of words, joining them up without the use of hyphens, turning the initial letter of the first word into a capital, and there, in an instant, you have a new word ready for inclusion in the dictionary. Inordinate length is no obstacle. What can you do with a language that has, for example, a word like *Hochseefischereiflottillenaktiengesellschaftsverwaltungsdirektionsassistentenstellvertretersgattin* and I dare say there are some even longer.

The result of translating these portmanteau-words into English must always be a phrase. Sometimes there are two or more alternatives, and so, if you do not find what you are looking for under one letter, try another likely one.

Acorn	*Eichel*
Adjutant . . .	*Adjutant*
Administration . .	*Verwaltung*
Aerodrome Supervision .	*Luftaufsichtdienst*
Aeroplane Observation Post	*Fliegerwache*
Aircraft Report Detachment	*Fluma (Flugmeldeabteilung)*

Aircraft Reporting Service	Flugmeldedienst
Air Force	Luftwaffe
Air Ministry	Reichsluftfahrtministerium
Air Reconnaissance	Luftaufklärung
Air Service Liaison Officer	Fliegerverbindungsoffizier
Air Warfare Training Establishment	Luftkriegsakademie
Air Zone Command	Luftgaukommando
Anchor	Anker
Anti-Aircraft Gun	Flak
Anti-Aircraft Protection	Flakschutz
Anti-Tank Defence	Panzerabwehr
Arm Badge	Armspiegel
Arm of the Service	Waffengattung
Armed Forces	Wehrmacht
Armoured Car, Tank	Panzerwagen
Army	Heer
Army Administration Department	Amtsverwaltungs-Departement
Army Corps H.Q.	Gruppenkommando
Army Ordnance Department	Heeres-Waffenamt
Artillery	Artillerie
Artillery Signal Unit	Artillerie-Verbindungs-Kommando
Artilleryman	Artillerist
Aspirant Officer	Offizier-anwärter
Badge	Abzeichen
Badge-Cloth	Abzeichentuch
Badges of Rank	Rankabzeichen
Bandmaster	Musikmeister
Bandsman	Spielmann
Bandsman's Epaulettes	Schwalbenester
Barracks	Kaserne

GLOSSARY

Battalion	*Bataillon*
Battery	*Batterie*
Bayonet	*Seitengewehr*
Belt	*Koppel*
Boot	*Schuh*
Braid	*Borte*
Breeches	*Stiefelhosen*
Buckle	*Schnalle*
Bugler	*Hornist*
Buttons	*Knöpfe*
Cadet	*Kadett*
Calibre	*Kaliber*
Cap	*Mütze*
Cap-band	*Besatzstreifen*
Cartridge Belt	*Patronengürtel*
Cavalry	*Kavallerie*
Cavalry Regiment	*Reiter-Regiment*
Chaplain (Army)	*Feldpfarrer*
Chief of the General Staff	*Chef des Generalstabes*
Chin-strap (Caps)	*Sturmriemen*
Cloak	*Umhang*
Cockade	*Kokarde*
Collar	*Kragen*
Collar-Patches	*Kragenpatten*
Colour distinguishing Service Arm	*Waffenfarbe*
Commander, Leader, Guide, Pilot, Driver	*Führer*
Commemoration Armlet	*Erinnerungsband*
Company	*Kompagnie*
Cord	*Schnur*
Cuff	*Aufschlag*
Cuff (of tunic, etc.)	*Ärmelaufschlag*
Dagger	*Dolch*

Defence Ordnance	*Sperrwaffen*
Details	*Einzelheiten*
District Command	*Bezirkskommando*
Dragoon	*Dragoner*
Driver	*Fahrer*
Drummer	*Tambour*
Education	*Bildung*
Engine	*Machine*
Engineer (Army)	*Pionier*
Engineer (Navy and Air Force)	*Ingenieur*
Ensigns (first stage)	*Fahnenjunker*
Ensigns (second stage)	*Fähnrich*
Ensigns (third stage)	*Oberfähnrich*
Epaulettes	*Epauletten*
Equipment	*Ausrüstung*
Executive Officer (Navy)	*See Offizier*
Experimental Laboratory	*Versuchsanstalt*
Farrier	*Beschlagschmied*
Fatigue Dress	*Arbeitsanzug*
Fatigue Party	*Arbeiterabteilung*
Field Cap	*Feldmütze*
Field Dress	*Feldanzug*
Field-grey	*Feldgrau*
Field Officer	*Stabsoffizier*
Field Service Boots	*Feldstiefel*
Field Service Tunic	*Waffenrock*
Fighter Command (Air Force)	*Jagdgeschwader*
Firefighting Service	*Feuerlöschdienst*
Flag, Colours, Standard	*Fahne*
Flying Service Dress	*Flugdienstanzug*
For Active Service	*Feldmarschmässig*
Forestry Official	*Forstbeamter*

GLOSSARY

Formation, Unit	*Formation*
Fortification	*Befestigung*
Fortress	*Festung*
Frog of a Bayonet, etc.	*Sabelschlaufe*
Gaiters, Leggings	*Gamaschen*
Garrison, Crew	*Besatzung*
Gloves	*Handschuhe*
Great-Coat	*Mantel*
Grenade	*Granate*
Government	*Regierung*
Guard, Sentry	*Wache*
Guard Duty	*Wachtdienst*
Guard Uniform	*Wachanzug*
Gun Captain (Machine-Gun)	*Gewehrführer*
Gun Detachment Personnel	*Bedienungsmannschaften (einer Batterie)*
Gun Layer	*Richtkanonier*
Half-Pay Officers	*zur Disposition*
Headquarters	*Stabsquartier*
High Command of the Armed Forces	*Oberkommando der Wehrmacht*
Hussar	*Husar*
Infantry	*Infanterie*
Infantry Regiment Signalling Detachment	*Ina (Nachrichtenmittelabteilung eines Infanterie Regiments)*
Infantry Soldier	*Infanterist*
Inspector-General	*Inspecteur*
Intendantur	*Commissariat*
Iron Cross	*Eisernes Kreuz*
Jacket	*Jacke*

Knapsack	Rücksack
Lanyard	Reissleine
Lapel	Brustklappe
Leave	Urlaub
Liaison Officer	Verbindungsoffizier
Life Guards	Leibgarde
Light Duty	Revierdienst
Listener	Horcher
Machine-Gun	Maschinengewehr
Marine Infantry Battalion	Seebataillon
Marksman	Meisterschütze
Marksman's Lanyard	Schützenabzeichen
Mechanic	Monteur
Mechanized Fighting Troops	Panzertruppen
Medical Corps	Sanitätskorps
Medical Officer	Arzt
Midshipman	Fähnrich
Military District	Wehrkreis
Military Law Official	Heeresjustizbeamter
Minister for Air	Reichsminister der Luftfahrt
Motor-Cyclist	Motorradfahrer
Mountain Guide (Military)	Heeresbergführer
Mountain Regiment	Gebirgs-regiment
National Emblem	Hoheitszeichen
Navy	Kriegsmarine
Non-Commissioned Officer	Unteroffizier ohne Portepee
N.C.O.s Stripe	Winkel
Oak-Leaves	Eichenlaube
Officer	Offizier
Officer's Sash	Schärpe
Officers' Examination	Offizierprüfung
Orderly Room, Office	Geschäftszimmer
Ordnance Department	Zeugamt

GLOSSARY

Ornament	*Spiegel*
Overcoat	*Mantel*
Parachute Troops	*Fallschirmtruppen*
Parade Dress	*Paradeanzug*
Paymaster	*Zahlmeister*
Petty Officer	*Maat*
Piece, Gun, Component Part.	*Stück*
Piping	*Vorstosz*
Pistol	*Pistole*
Platoon	*Zug*
Quartermaster	*Quartiermeister (Army)*
Rangefinder	*Entfernungsmesser*
Rank Badge	*Dienstgradabzeichen*
Reconnaissance	*Aufklärung*
Recruit	*Rekrut*
Recruiting Authorities	*Ersatzbëhorden*
Re-employed Retired Officer	*Ergänzungsoffizier*
Regimental Signalling Officer	*Namo (Nachrichtenmittel-Offizier)*
Regulation	*Vorschrift*
Remount	*Remonted*
Reporting Uniform	*Meldeanzug*
Research Department	*Untersuchungsamt*
Reserve	*Beurlaubstand*
Reserves identified with a District	*Landwehr*
Retired	*ausser Dienst (a.D.)*
Retired	*Verabschiedet*
Rifle Battery	*Gewehrbatterie*
Rifleman	*Jäger*
Sabre	*Sabel*

Sailor	*Matrose*
Seam, edge	*Naht*
Searchlight equipment	*Scheinwerfergerät*
Service Dress	*Dienstanzug*
Ship	*Schiff*
Shoe	*Halbschuh*
Shoulder Cord	*Schulterschnur*
Shoulder-strap	*Schulterklappe*
Side-arm Tassels	*Troddeln, Faustriemen; Portepees*
Signal Corps	*Nachrichtentruppe*
Ski	*Schi*
Sleeve Patches	*Armelpatten*
Smoke troops	*Nebeltruppen*
Socks	*Socken*
Soldier	*Soldat*
Spurs	*Sporen*
Squadron	*Schwadron, Staffel (Air Force)*
Staff	*Stab*
Staff College	*Kriegs-Akademie*
Staff Sergeant of Artillery Technical Establishments	*Obermeister*
Steel Helmet	*Stahlhelm*
Step	*Stufe*
Strong Ticking	*Drillich*
Supplementary Reservists	*Ergänzungsmannschaften*
Supply Office or Depot	*Proviantamt*
Supreme Court of Justice of the *Wehrmacht*	*Reichskriegsgericht*
Supreme Head of the Armed Forces	*Oberster Befehlshaber der Wehrmacht*
Swastika	*Hakenkreuz*
Sword	*Schwert*
Sword (Short) used as Bayonet	*Faschinenmesser*
Sword Belt	*Degenkoppel*

GLOSSARY

Torpedo	*Torpedo*
Tradition Unit	*Stammtruppenteil*
Transport Squadron	*Fahreskadron*
Trench Mortar	*Minenwerfer*
Troddel Shaft	*Stengel*
Troops	*Truppen*
Trousers	*Beinkleider*
Trumpeter	*Trompeter*
Turret Gun	*Turmkanone*
Uniform Peaked Cap	*Schirmmütze*
Unit	*Truppenteil*
Veterinary Corps	*Veterinärwesen*
Waist-Belt (Officers)	*Feldbinde*
Waistcoat	*Weste*
Walking-Out Dress	*Ausgehanzug*
War Ministry	*Kriegsministerium*
Warrant Officer	*Unteroffizier mit Portepee*
Watchkeeping Officer (Navy)	*Wachhabende Offizier*
Waterproof	*Gummimantel*
Wellington Boot	*Schaftstiefel*
Wind Jacket	*Windjacke*
Wings	*Schwingen*

www.ingramcontent.com/pod-product-compliance
Ingram Content Group UK Ltd.
Pitfield, Milton Keynes, MK11 3LW, UK
UKHW021256180426
11947UKWH00011B/803